Praise for

"With tremendous faith and a transparent heart this book inspires, lifts and reminds us of God's mercy, forgiveness, and grace!"

Pastor Robert J. Lowe,
New Beginnings C.O.G.I.C. Buffalo, New York

"Linda Meadows brings the relevancy of 'today' in her book *The Blessedness of Believing: A Devotional Journey of Life's Lessons* and God's Promises. Her devotions are universal, timeless, and spiritual; and exemplify her humor, warmth, passion and caring. She brings to life the people, things and places she has observed and shares them compassionately with her readers."

Dr. Calvin H. Sydnor III
Editor, The Christian Recorder
The Official Newspaper of the A.M.E. Church

"As a hospital chaplain, when I hear the varied stories of people's lives I always wonder 'Where's God in all of this?' *The Blessedness of Believing* answers that question unequivocally. No matter what challenges you're facing, God's right in the middle of it (with you), just waiting to be acknowledged and trusted! Journeying with author Linda Meadows through her life's lessons became a journey down memory lane through my own life and the lessons I've learned, and enabled me to celebrate that I was never really on the path alone."

Rev. Audrey L. Pryor-Mouizi

"There is a time for everything and a season for every activity under heaven" (Ecclesiastes 3:1 NIV). The season is now for this work by Linda Meadows. Mrs. Meadows has captured God's voice as he leads and guides her daily and summarized her journey with GOD through the language in these devotionals. You can hear her melodious voice and visualize those whom she writes about, because these devotionals are everyone's story. Come read and enjoy, as we walk in Linda's garden of life."

Stephanie Williams Torres, Esq.

the blessedness of
BELIEVING

the blessedness of
BELIEVING

a daily devotional of life's lessons & God's promises

LINDA MOSE MEADOWS

Tate Publishing & Enterprises

Published by Tate Publishing & Enterprises, LLC
127 E. Trade Center Terrace | Mustang, Oklahoma 73064 USA
1.888.361.9473 | www.tatepublishing.com

Tate Publishing is committed to excellence in the publishing industry. The company reflects the philosophy established by the founders, based on Psalms 68:11,
"The Lord gave the word and great was the company of those who published it."

Book design copyright © 2007 by Tate Publishing, LLC. All rights reserved.
Cover design by Elizabeth A. Mason
Interior design by Lynly D. Taylor

Published in the United States of America

ISBN: 978-1-60247-514-4
07.07.20

Acknowledgments

I know just what you're thinking. What is this commentary about? This is supposed to be a short and sweet acknowledgement. That's what my husband Ricky said, but often we agree to disagree. That makes for great peace. It's just how it goes, just like our personal journeys that stretch us, challenge us, bewilder us, and surprise us. God views our experiences in one light and we see it totally in a different light. And often if you are like me, it takes many more experiences that turn into weeks, months, sometimes years long before we get the essence of that life's lesson.

My life's entire journey has been marked with some outstanding individuals: My beloved grandparents Ellsworth Jackson, Ruth Jackson and Rita Mose, my wonderful siblings John Mose, Jr.; Steven Mose and Eric Mose, Roland and Robin Edwards, Aunt Shirley and Uncle Joseph Mose, Bishop Dwight and Sister Renee' Brown, Elder Matthew Brown, Elder Robert and Tonia Lowe, Bishop Vashti Murphy McKenzie, Bishop T. Anthony Bronner, Rev. Kenneth Q. James, Evangelist Wilma Taylor, Rev. Edward and Minister Sheilah Olds, Franco and Deidre Accornero, Minister Kenneth Jackson, Dr. Calvin Sydnor, Rev. Dr. Timothy Tee Boddie, my wonderful parents John O. Mose Sr. and Clarinda Jackson Mose, Leonard Pleasant, Dr. Cameron Byrd, Arthur "Jackie" and Vivian Reed, Aunt Queenie Young, Minister Raymonia Mitchell, Bertha Boston, Dr. Murray and Sherry Spain, Dennis and Marita Daniels, Marion Brinkley-Bouie, Dr. Allen Lewis, Curtis and Deidre Steed, Dr. Sheila Greenlee, Dr. Robert and Amanda Murray, Evelyn R. Smith, Dr. Charles Ponquinette, Emily Ruff, Larry & Jackie Curtis, Andre and Sakinah Garcia, Papa and Mama Bailey, Cassandra Burney, Dr. William James Marshall, Girija Venkat, Dr. Peter Wherry,

Mother Pauline McCant, Mother Lula Caruthers, Cheryl Reid-Williams, Beverly McCant and Minister Anita McCant, Josephine Hayes, Rev. George & Marlene Bright, Gene and Maime Credle, Minister Ronnette Williams, Verlaine Quinney, Deacons Lebron and Frances Jackson, Helen Brooks, Ronald and Deborah Witherspoon, Sheila Allen, Patricia Whitaker, Shaw University, Newsome-Askew Family (wonderful cousins: Leta, Lee, both Leon's, Hawletta and Marvola), The Nedab Family: Mother Margaret Nedab, Cathy Gaskins-Nedab, Mother Queen Hunter and Kaye Nedab, Lessie Bowser-Warton, Anna Bell, Nicole Crews, Orin and Camille Jefferson, Edward and Jean Herndon. My New Mount Ararat Temple of Prayer Family and Mother's Board. Fondly remembering: Bailey Avenue AME Zion, Lincoln Memorial United Methodist Church, Elim Fellowship Family, The Blackett Family, Queen Street Baptist Church and Herbert Baptist Church Families. All my brother and sister friends who are my family too. The Aljuwani Family (Mileka, Hasheem, Shakoor and Wahab Jr.) and all my church mothers and fathers, my sweet in-laws Willa Cobb, the Thornton's and Huckabee's, Zina Mose, Miranda Mose, Mary Meadows (the sweetest mommie-in-law), Tonie Poole, Veronica "Ronnie" and Willie Ray, Richard Meadows, Sr. God planted them in my life for a reason. For that I am grateful. For you, I am truly grateful.

Surely understand there are so many names of friends, loved ones, surrogate mothers, fathers, uncles, brothers and sisters like: Abla 'Michele' Kekeh, Maria Santos, Dr. Elder Barbara Mattai, Ruth Gallman, Minister Renita Shadwick, Darlene Varlack, Tanisha Zeigler, Rev. Joreatha Barrett, Rev. Audrey L. Pryor-Mouizi, Millie Aven, Janie Spence, Anita Dixon, Senior Services of Southeastern VA. and my Hampton University friends, Stephanie Torres, Esq. and David and Jeanette Snead, Andrea Mujihad, Esq., Minister April Barber, Esther Miles,

Stephanie Barber, Douglas and Donna Darrell, Donna Byrd, Tracy Johnson, Brenda McKenzie, Mary White, Sheila Reed, Benay Legree, Harriette Taylor, Marion Shakir, Rosemary Vinnie, Lenora Gunter, Rosa Bundick, Veronica Johnson, Sala, Dorothy Wagstaff-Williams 'Princess Photography', Barbara Copeland, Ruby Jackson, Minister Martin Bundick, Jerome Shadwick, Elton Barber, Minister Reginald and Martha Burt, Minister Mark and Pamela Johnson, Deacon Johnnie and Cheryl Davis, Rev. Anthony and Katherine Brown and Minister James and Delores Giles- thank God for your circle of love, outpouring of gifts, prayers and words of encouragement. My beloved nieces, nephews, God-children and our children; you were always there for me whether it was your physical presence, or prayers you silently said on my behalf, we grew in faith together. Your love was never far away.

Our Heavenly Father is so remarkable. I thank God that daily I can witness the love of Jesus because of how you've all impacted my life. I know of our Father's mighty love because I know you.

Oh! The scripture rings true that proclaims we have Jesus the Great High Priest who also loves us. Take a look with me:

> "Let us, then, hold firmly to the faith we profess. For we have a great High Priest who has gone into the very presence of God—Jesus, the Son of God. Our High Priest is not one who cannot feel sympathy for our weaknesses. On the contrary, we have a High priest who was tempted in every way that we are, but did not sin. Let us have confidence, then, and approach God's throne where there is grace. There we receive mercy and find grace to help us just when we need it."
> (Hebrews 4:14–16)

May our Lord and Savior continue to keep and bless all of you.

Grandparents: Ellsworth Calvin & Evelyn Ruth Jackson
Family Reunion

1932

TABLE OF CONTENTS

FOREWORD

What do we do when troubles arrive, when crises happen, when our hearts are broken, when disappointments settle into our place of being, or more generally, when we are in a state of turmoil? What can bring us relief and restore our peace? For believers in Christ, it is the word of God, and it is the testimonies or shared experiences of those who have encountered what we are presently feeling and have emerged triumphantly.

In *The Blessedness of Believing*, Linda Meadows has allowed us to enter into a portion of her world and has courageously and with unadulterated honesty shared her struggles, challenges and triumphs. She has brought us the comfort of knowing we are not alone in feeling those things which we are sometimes too ashamed to admit, and has encouraged us in knowing that we are indeed overcomers; without a doubt, the victory is ours.

The Blessedness of Believing is poignant, honest, and sometimes funny, introspective reflections straight from the heart. It is accounts of situations with which we can all identify, and it provides a challenge for us to become all that we are destined to be, to persevere until we see the promised victory. These anecdotes deal with real issues and truths about real life feelings and experiences; her moments become ours. They incite within us feelings of nostalgia, contentment and eager anticipation of the triumph that is certain to belong to us. The accompanying prayers get straight to the heart of the matter and right to the situation and need. Upon reading the accounts, you feel the scriptures, the word of God, have been given meaning by coming alive in your life. Your heart is renewed, your spirit is refreshed, and your determination is revived. Praise God!

Dr. Barbara Huddleston-Mattai,
Professor, Buffalo State and Evangelist,
New Mt. Ararat Temple of Prayer

PREFACE

There have been more moments in my life than I care to admit that I felt it would be easier to throw my hands up and say *forget this!* Forget this blended family business, forget these financial struggles, forget one personal sacrifice after another and forget living like God wants me! But, oh no, friends, *I believe! I believe that love conquers all and answers when you call!* Those words are from BeBe Winans' song on his CD entitled *BeBe Live and Up Close.* That's my song as well.

I believe God for everything! And on days when I act like I don't understand, God opens my eyes to new scripture, speaks to my husband's heart and he shares a genuine token of love. God also provides enlightenment through moving lyrics; loved ones' encouraging words, letting me hear a prophetic word and continuing to allow me to experience the benefit of his grace and mercy.

I have discovered the *Blessedness of Believing.* I have experienced this for myself. My journey began before I knew myself. God knows all about me. He knows my challenges, my fears, and my heart's desire. Like you, I am learning and evolving into who God has purposed me to be. If I give up and "forget this" faith journey and walk away, then I, not God, fail. It's all part of His divine plan that I love, and yes, sometimes suffer through, get through and pray through trials, successes and set backs. We are never failures when we stumble, walk, crawl, fall flat on our faces because we choose to hold on and *live by faith, not sight.* Instead of talking negatively to myself, my journey has me often quoting a scripture my mother loves; it is now one of my favorites.

Eye hath not seen, nor ear heard, neither have entered into the heart of man the things that God hath prepared for those that love Him. I Corinthians 2:9 NIV

I can't help but marvel at how God has matured me. My reliance is totally on Jesus. God has done everything His way from my marriage to my then unemployment and reemployment at *my hearts desire*—Hampton University. My life is far from a fairy tale existence. I have experienced the full gamut of emotions. Then something happened. My focus had to change from what I was feeling to what God would have me experience. My husband encouraged me to write and spread some inspiration. What did I have to say? I could not have imagined that a few devotionals written as an act of encouragement for those visiting the Queen Street Baptist Church's Website would evolve into a book.

These writings validated for me that God is active, alive, loves me and cares about what concerns me.

God had done it once again, taken a little and made a lot. Just like our mothers and grandmothers who emptied the refrigerator of all the leftovers and created a sumptuous stew that feeds many and provides leftovers for several days, God has stretched me similarly in the same manner.

Many of these devotionals were written while I sat cramped in a tight broom closet-like cubicle. I would start my day with scriptures and other inspirational readings to help me stay anchored. His word would become crystal clear. My own story and devotional would be born.

As I wrote my story, my devotional, I would experience a flood of emotions and revisit some painful episodes in my life that I wasn't prepared to think about at work, and surely I didn't want to revisit those times and share them in a devotional. I now realize that God thought differently. He made me ask myself, "How can we, faith-filled, Bible-quoting Christians possibly be of encouragement to others if we pretend that all is well, all the time, and Jesus hasn't done a thing?" Oh sure! I was blessed but there was a boatload of stress. I struggled through many writings but Jesus was with me every step of the way and encouraged me to share them with you. He continued to be there with me during that bewildering personal season of unemployment and my stepchildren living with us.

If not another soul says a kind or encouraging word to you, tell yourself that *God will never leave nor forsake you!* Trust me friends, I have had to go back and revisit my writings. Clearly, God said, *Linda, go back and take your own medicine.* That was hard to swallow because sometimes, one just wants to languish in the disappointment and hurt. But I am convinced that our pain and joy serve a great purpose in our lives. If we allow God to minister to us during those times, we'll be freer than we've ever imagined.

The more one reads the Holy Scripture the closer one walks with God. Daily, I am struggling and learning through life's lessons, but I fully understand that God is in charge. Dr. Peter Wherry, Pastor of Queen Street Baptist Church (Norfolk, Virginia) reminded me of that plain truth during Sunday's worship service.

Come on friends! Let's journey together in *the Blessedness of Believing* and be assured that whether it is sunshine or rain; Jesus Christ has a conversation and an answer for all we face.

DELIGHTING IN GOD'S PROMISES

"…then you will find your joy in the LORD, and I will cause you to ride on the heights of the land and to feast on the inheritance of your father Jacob. The mouth of the LORD has spoken."

Isaiah 8:14

When heavy rain and storms occur in our lives it is easy to succumb to the negative weather report. The report forecasts setbacks and heartaches—these things are just as they appear—gloomy, hopeless with no relief in sight! But as believers in the Gospel of Jesus Christ, we don't have to believe the dismal report. We have another report—a report of promise, a report of love and a good report that reminds us to delight in all of God's promises. Today let's smile at what appears to be a dismal report and know that we have something so much more precious that will shelter us from life's storms. Let's journey and see what God has to say on this rainy day.

What a wet and gray morning this was, or so it appeared to be. The raindrops were thick and cool. I opened my patio door to see and test what the weather was like. I needed to know what I'd have to wear (hopefully no heavy coats). I now know I need my umbrella. I couldn't put my hands on, could not find it. No umbrella this morning. My little red umbrella was missing.

That did not stop me. Instead, I wore my green hooded jacket, which surprisingly acted as a shield from the elements. The material my jacket is made of provides great insulation and the hood is big enough to actually cover my eyes. So, I was ready to make it today, despite the elements outside. That's just like our Father's promises.

Isaiah 58 speaks of true fasting, but more importantly it addresses the results of our obedience to our heavenly Father. Please read it for your self.

> "The Lord will guide you always; he will satisfy your needs in a sun scorched land and will strengthen your frame."
>
> Isaiah 58:11

The scripture further states in verse 11 that your obedience to God will "...be like a well-watered garden, like a spring whose water never fails."

Can't you just picture that? In our letting go of carnal, rebellious behavior and insistence on doing things your own way, verse 14 points out:

Then you will find your joy in the Lord, and I will cause you to ride on the heights of the land and to feast on the inheritance of your father Jacob. The mouth of the Lord has spoken.

Don't you just love it! It's like my jacket. We are protected, and yes most assuredly we are covered in God's promises when we delight in Jesus Christ.

THE POWER OF LOVE

"Love is patient, love is kind. It does not envy, it does not boast, it is not proud. It is not rude, it is not self-seeking, it is not easily angered, it keeps no record of wrongs. Love does not delight in evil but rejoices with the truth. It always protects, always trusts, always hopes, always perseveres."

I Corinthians 13:4–7

I sure do miss my loved ones that have gone on to glory. Do you ever stop in the middle of your day and snicker or smile to yourself, because the memory of a loved one is so clear? You can hear their voices, the little clips in their sentences, the way they pause or loved a familiar saying like: *This too shall pass!* Or, *Baby let me tell you this one thing!* There was a special way they might roll sounds together. You just feel their presence and know they were so full of life.

Some of those loved ones for me were Mama Bailey (Agnes Bailey), Big Mama (Irene Harris), Grandma Dixie (Dixie Johnson), and Big Daddy (George Harris). Big Daddy was full of knowledge. My brothers and I loved visiting them. Their houses were filled with love. It grabbed you and as soon as you hit their doorstep, the mixture of smells filled our nostrils and pleasantly greeted us. Good cooking, baking, perfumes and ointments. When we journeyed into Big Daddy's basement, it was a new world of discovery-memorabilia from world travels, posters and black and white photos of when he was a boxer and listening to his treasured 33's and 45's of operas (never in English). He amazed us with his ability to speak German and French. I didn't tell you he was also a pastor and a teacher. What a delight it was to listen to his stories. Their spirits live on.

Mama Bailey provides those tremendous memories for my son in his youth and me in my adulthood. Sometimes out of the *blue* my son will say, "Mom, I miss Mama Bailey!" Then we chuckle together about a fond memory we have of her. I know he's been touched by her love. Mama Bailey was wonderful to us; actually I met the Bailey's through my younger brother. The Bailey's became our extended family; we shared good meals, holidays, birthdays and anniversary celebrations. We comforted each other during difficult times. I remember sitting on her bed and talking with her during one of her terrible bouts with cancer. It had reoccurred. She cried on my shoulder and said, "You know you are my baby." Do you have any idea what that meant to me as a woman, I too am a mother. For many years prior to that she fought her illnesses with dignity. She loved the Lord and wasn't bashful about sharing and giving her love.

It was nothing to wrap up home made cookies and ham to take to the sick and shut-in. If a college student was struggling, she helped. I called her an undercover missionary because she never made a "big to do" about giving and showing her love. She did just as Jesus instructed us,

> "Therefore encourage one another and build each other up, just as in fact you are doing."
>
> I Thessalonians 5:11

Whenever anyone in the family was depressed or suffering, Mama Bailey was a source of comfort and inspiration. She was a true daughter of Rizpah. She did not hide or pretend that things didn't exist. Candor was her middle name.

This woman of God (along with so many other loved ones)

demonstrated true Christian service and love. Are you a blessing to someone because of the genuine kindness and love shown? Chicken soup, greens, Holy Ghost spirit-filled encouraging words, kisses on the forehead, and warm hugs are loving touches needed by all of us. The scripture reminds us that Jesus spoke and calmed the storm. You too have the power of love in your bosom. Calm someone's storm with your love.

> "Love is patient and kind; love is not jealous or boastful; it is not arrogant or rude. Love does not insist on its own way; it is not irritable or resentful; it does not rejoice at wrong, but rejoices in the right. Love bears all things, believes all things, and hopes all things. Love never fails."
>
> I Corinthians 13:4

You become a "Mama Bailey" or a "Big Daddy" in someone's life and don't hold back your love. You'll be such a blessing. Have a good day.

A Change of Heart

"For if, by the trespass of the one man, death reigned through that one man, how much more will those who receive God's abundant provision of grace and of the gift of righteousness reign in life through the one man, Jesus Christ."

Romans 5:17

Last week my husband, with a gift of worship, gave me a CD, it surprised me. Now you know we all benefit from my gift, but that's how it goes. I love and appreciate the gift and the giver. I was immediately blessed with the upbeat songs of praise and encouraging words spoken. The recording artist, her arms outstretched on the cover. She is in worship; deep worship and you can experience the peace that resonates from her posture. When I take the opportunity to stop and listen to this CD, there is one particular song that I truly enjoy.

The melody says: "Show me your ways, Lord, that I may walk with you. My very hope is you…Show me your ways Lord, that I may talk with you…"

(Be mindful the words might not be in that order. Sometimes I get the words turned around. That doesn't stop me). But, this is what I really wanted to share with you.

Today I tried to really understand what our Father was relaying to me, regarding, counting myself dead to sin and being alive and seeing the power of Christ in my life. Clarity came. My worship CD song "Show Me Your Way Lord" came to mind. The melody just welled up and I began to hum it joyfully. It was not she singing, it was now my voice, my song. That doesn't always happen, but I am convinced that because I pushed my personal preoccupations aside and my work-to-do list, and for a moment—stopped so that God, our Father could get through. The devotional text is:

> "All who receive God's wonderful, gracious gift of righteousness will live triumphant over sin and death through this one man Jesus Christ."
>
> Romans 5:17

As God is showing me and talking with me in scripture and song, it's sinking in this morning that I can live triumphantly in spite of _____. (You fill in the blank.) We have a new resurrected life in Christ. Have a blessed day.

In Spite of Myself

"Whom have I in heaven but you? And earth has nothing I desire besides you. My flesh and my heart may fail, but God is the strength of my heart and my portion forever."

Psalms 73:25,26

My prayer at this very moment should be:

Lord Jesus, in spite of myself and my little concerns, you did bless me today and on countless other occasions. Forgive me for being oblivious of your love and goodness. Lord Jesus, in spite of my heaviness of heart, you still love me. Thank you. Lord Jesus, in spite of what I can not forecast, you have it all under control! I am thankful. Lord Jesus, in spite of all of life's setbacks I find myself in; your word says never will you leave nor forsake me. Thank you for your Mercy. Lord in spite of it all, you are our saving grace. In the matchless name of your marvelous son Christ Jesus. Hallelujah! Lord Jesus, yours is a sustaining presence and power. Your word says, my beloved is mine and I am His. I am blessed. Thank you, Lord.

That's just what was in my spirit to pray. Moments before my husband phoned me at work, I had been feeling perplexed and just tired. Earlier that morning, I had written a check and the balance was bleak. The monthly expenses exceeded our budget. I needed to have a good cry; a shoulder to lean on and caring, comforting arms to assure me. I was at work. I immediately thought to myself, "Linda, pull it together." I better not shed a tear, nor look as though I was not about "office business." You know that look that says, "I don't have time to chat, there's a report due!" Instead I e-mailed a friend who had forwarded me an earlier message. God knows how to take care of you. He reminded me that this friend knew about the power of prayer, knew that life's heaviness could become a tidal wave. This friend would accept all I had to say and not belittle or question my faith. That's all I could stand at that moment.

Do you remember the great gospel legend James Cleveland? Well, he spoke about feeling heaviness in your spirit and then sang, "Nobody told me that the road would be easy, Lord I've come too far from where I started from, I don't believe you brought me this far to leave me." Today that's my song.

For all of us in this precarious place of "in spite of" know without a shadow of a doubt, that our Jesus assures us that (your and my) flesh and heart faileth;

> "…but God is the strength of my heart, and my por-
> tion forever."

Psalm 73:26

Friends, have you ever heard your pastor say, "This word was for me?" Today, I have a clear understanding of that. Be blessed and encouraged on this faith journey.

BLESSED ASSURANCE

"Then the man said, 'Lord, I believe' and he worshiped him."

John 9:38

My brother John came rushing through my mind. I could see him—so full of life, animated and moving his hands and passionate about what he's saying. Sometimes he gets so tickled at what he's saying that he starts laughing before he's completed his sentence. We are eleven months apart. As long as I've known him, I've known myself. I have four brothers so you can imagine how loud our home was. We all had something to say. We call my brother, John, *Johnny*. He's a junior and will deny that he's anything like my dad in looks or behavior. We all know differently, but that is not a bad thing. When we tease him, I believe he thinks we think it is. That's our inside joke. Growing up folks always would say things like "I know you're spoiled." Well, quite the contrary, I am the oldest and only girl. There was lots of responsibility given to the oldest. I thought that gave me certain *bossing rights* and privileges. My mother would often tell me I was in charge. When my parents left me in charge, no one seemed to know even if I threatened anyone with tattling.

My mom would continue to assure me of my authority. I'm convinced she knew they were hardheads. Those fun loving brothers are now fathers and husbands. Now they all live far from me—but are close in my heart.

As I'm sitting here at my desk, listening to Anita Baker sing the lyrics "Sometimes you win, sometimes you lose," Johnny jumped into my spirit. He is an admirable young man. I remember when he had a desire to leave a lucrative position and start his own business. There were more naysayers than supporters—he treated them as though they had no authority—he embraced what he dreamed and now loves his independence in being his own boss. He contributes a weekly health and fitness article to a Fort Worth community newspaper. Imagine a 'fitness guru" who loves the Negro Leagues memorabilia. Ask him anything regarding one of the leagues and he can rattle all kinds of facts and figures. He's a broad thinker—knows how to negotiate. But more importantly he really knows how to lend a helping hand. He has been there for us when we needed him. He is a blessed assurance.

> Our Heavenly Father will do that—I'm convinced, He'll plant loved ones in our midst who can lend a helping hand and provide us with more than a lecture and pat on the back. God assures us that in the midst of turmoil and trouble he'll be our anchor and sustainer. Remember Jesus said, "I will not leave you comfortless, I will come to you."
>
> John 14:18

Just when I phoned my brother in distress, he was able to help. Encouragement was delivered from Texas to my door in Virginia Beach. My faith is restored over and over again. *Lord, I believe.*

Our, Most High God will work instantly in our loneliness, confusion, despair, discomfort, disjointed relationships, dysfunction and dismay. And most certainly, in our joy and peace, He resides there too. We have a blessed Assurance in the Father, Son and Holy Ghost that we are loved and not alone. I pray that out of His glorious riches He may strengthen you with power through His Spirit in your inner being…(Ephesians 3:16).

Have a good day.

A Heart Conversation

"I will fear no evil; for you are with me; Your rod and your staff, they comfort me"

Psalm 23:4

Can we talk for a moment? Have you had the opportunity to be in a supermarket or waiting on the bus, in the Motor Vehicles Department line or just taking a leisurely walk through your neighborhood—when out of no where comes a stranger and these folks begin to share information? It's as though you are old friends and it's okay for them to start in the middle of a thought. Before you realize it, you might become enticed into a conversation.

My husband says I have a magnet that draws these folks. They often share what's heavy on their hearts; much of it is personal information. As you listen, you don't know when to stop them or if you even should so you smile, nod your head occasionally, but secretly wish they would stop talking. You honestly feel overwhelmed and intruded upon. I've even witnessed these persons speaking to someone else and others are embarrassed by the conversations and they try to back away—ever so politely of course.

I am often approached in my most favorite spot, the thrift store. Yes, I absolutely love treasure hunting at the thrift stores, usually alone. Those of us that are passionate about hunting in the thrift stores don't want to be disturbed—it's sacred time. So how do we handle this awkwardness? I'm not sure that there's a standard answer. Why does that disturb us? Especially those of us who love the Lord and aren't ashamed of the gospel? I remember what we were taught...*don't speak to strangers*. Certainly, you can-

LINDA MOSE MEADOWS

not be too careful. But, could it possibly be that we have a light within us that illuminates wherever we are? Even with our hands digging and sorting treasures. As Christians, many of us shy away from *heart* conversations. You know those *heart* conversations of areas in our lives we don't want to discuss or topics that can trigger conversations, because it's risky. We open ourselves up for the unexpected, then what? But our reality as lovers and worshippers of Jesus Christ—we don't have to live in fear and be thrown off guard by someone needing to converse.

> "You are the light of the world. A city on a hill cannot be hidden. Neither do people light a lamp and put it under a bowl. Instead they put it on its stand, and it gives light to everyone in the house. In the same way, let your light shine before men, that they may see your good deeds and praise your Father in heaven."
>
> Matthew 5:14, 16

Our Holy Scripture reminds us to let our lights shine, so that men may see our good works and become drawn not so much to us, but the divine light that dwells in us because of our relationship—a deep love relationship that we have with Christ.

Many strangers are drawn because of the compassionate Jesus that lives in you and me. It's all over you! So, yes be ever so careful when you are moving out and about but, sometimes God gives you the opportunity to listen and share in a *heart* conversation. It really has nothing to do with you but, everything to do with Jesus. Some lonely soul might benefit from hearing from Him—and at that moment in time, it can only come through you. Remind them of God's protection and assurance that:

"When you pass through the waters, I will be with you; and when you pass through the rivers, they will not sweep over you. When you walk through the fire, you will not be burned; the flames will not set you ablaze."

Isaiah 43:2

May God continue His good work in you.

Persevering, While Waiting On the Promises

"For my thoughts are not your thoughts, neither are your ways my ways, declares the LORD. As the heavens are higher than the earth, so are my ways higher than your ways and my thoughts than your thoughts."

Isaiah 55:8–9

I know that we'd like to have a handle on believing that we have ourselves together and know just how our lives will pan out. Admittedly, I have prayed, petitioned God about how to do and deliver what I needed with explicit instructions. And imagine we'd like to think if we pray the "right" prayer, combine and let our commands flow in a certain fashion, God will deliver. God will deliver, but oh friends never on my terms, nor yours. He sees the entire pie, we just know who baked it. I am learning that God's thoughts are so much higher than mine and like you, am being blessed in the process.

Late yesterday our package finally arrived in the Norfolk area. Keem, our eldest son came through the door and announced that Federal Express said that we have to go to their office or they will deliver it tomorrow. Never mind that our package had been delivered to the wrong address. This was only discovered after we phoned Federal Express to inquire about "package destination." So, mothers you know how we pipe up and say things like, "It's only fair that the delivery of our package arrive promptly!" No one cared about that soapbox announcement. My husband and son went to get our package. You ask, what was in the package?

Buffalo Wings of course! You wonder why this is such a big deal? Only when you travel home with us will you understand! Ask any Buffalonian, wings are a taste sensation. The Chamber of Commerce would only have to ask me once to do a promo. Mind you, our wings have been arriving for several days now; Federal Express has never been so slow. I thought the key word with them was express?

Keem is our adopted son; actually he's the son of our beloved friends, the Browns. Now that Keem has relocated to Norfolk, we claim him as ours. A young man of great faith, lots of perseverance, not to mention, he's kind. I often remind him that he believes he's here to attend Norfolk State and I think…*God had so much more in store.* Keem is a role model for my son and often is unaware of it. It was Keem's generosity that got those wings shipped from Buffalo to Norfolk. Recently, he visited Buffalo and went directly to the restaurant to place the order. Our family was pumped, we were psyched!

I envisioned a delivery square box with barbecued pit wings slightly tinged from the charcoal grill, drenched, smothered in sauce; not to leave out the containers of blue cheese and a sprinkling of carrot sticks and celery. When my husband and son walked that "box" through the door, that's not how it was "voila." The restaurant had the nerve to send a T-shirt with their logo (weren't they smart? Free advertising) and two frozen food bags that resembled wings from any body's super market. They teased us with a beautiful brochure containing preparation instructions.

Inside the box were two containers of frozen blue cheese dressing. *Zapping the containers in the microwave—so unwise!* Before I knew it, I roared with laughter. I thought, *There must be a lesson in this.* At the time I was not sure. I didn't know what we'd receive but it certainly was not this!

In my contemplation this morning, I realized that's often the case in our journey with Jesus. No matter your station in life we are perplexed about what didn't go the way we expected it would. I am sure that you too have often painted an elaborate mental picture of what a certain outcome should be and reality presented you something like our chicken wing escapade! I was sure that when our package arrived that the Federal Express deliveryman was not going to be able to stand it and have tasted at least three wings! Do you think God has a great sense of humor? I sure do. Jesus reminds us that He knows the plans he has to prosper us and not harm us. Check your concordance. It's in there.

Friends, while you are waiting on God's promises in your marriage, your faith walk, your health encounter, your parenting unruly and uncooperative children, your loving difficult people and whatever else you are currently challenged with, be encouraged as you persevere. Jesus just might have something else in mind for you. Remember:

> "Let us draw near to God with a sincere heart in full assurance of faith, having our hearts sprinkled to cleanse us from a guilty conscience and having our bodies washed with pure water. Let us hold unswervingly to the hope we profess, for he who promised is faithful."
>
> Hebrews 10:22–23

Have a blessed day!

Mustard Seed Faith

"He replied, 'because you have so little faith. I tell you the truth, if you have faith as small as a mustard seed, you can say to this mountain, Move from here to there and it will move. Nothing will be impossible for you…'"

Matthew 17:20

I've introduced you to our eldest son, Keem. I enjoy sharing Keem stories with you because his faith moves are sobering and he's a young man whose life demonstrates how awesome our Jesus is. He didn't grow up in a home with Betty Crocker and Ward Clever. Life was hard. But despite that, Keem is so proud to be attending Norfolk State University. I know that it has everything to do with his prayer which God has answered.

"He put a new song in [Keem's] mouth, a hymn of praise to [his] God"

Psalm 40:3

He's reaching a goal that has been deep within his heart for such a long time. This was a dream he had pushed to the side for a moment. He did not come directly from high school to college. Other events in his life took precedence over college, but he held on to the hope. One day he decided and said, "I've had enough," and drove to Norfolk and enrolled in college. I am sure you've inferred that Keem is determined, and has aspirations.

His previously deferred dreams are now being realized. He's equally pumped up about being a "Spartan" and playing football.

The opposing team is in for it. Often we will start conversing on one matter and invariably "talk football." Lovers of football speak another language. Theirs is a language of passion about "executed" plays or formations that are either mind blowing or down right dismal. I honestly don't have a clue, but love to tease my son and interject something I heard a sports commentator say just to poke fun and get a good laugh. Then my son might say, "Ma, what did you think of that game last night?" Then he's got me, the jokes on me. I am now learning football and what area on the field each of the players is responsible for. Imagine there's more to football than a field goal and touch down.

During high school, Keem had established a positive relationship with his coach. His coach could see this young man's tenacity and determination. This coach motivated and often encouraged Keem to speak up and share with other team mates the truth about a practice or game. This occurred on the bus trip home after a lost game. The coach noticed Keem upset and crying and questioned him.

The coach said, "You've played well, what are you crying for?" Keem stated that his teammates played like they expected to lose. Keem further revealed that the night before the playoffs he had looked forward to winning and on the big game day played that way. Keem interjected that his teammates were doing something different. The night before the big game, the star player was anticipating losing and he played that way during game time.

When this was shared with me during lunch, I screamed with delight! Didn't that just hit your spirit? How in life we do that—expect to loose! We often have our winning "game faces" on—but in reality, we have already concluded that we have no chance of succeeding. Our mind set is one of defeatism and consequently our life's dreams are never realized. Our movement throughout life becomes self-fulfilling prophecies. Where's our mustard seed faith? We can turn the games of life around.

This morning know that you know it's time for a new mindset. God is doing a new thing in all believers of the gospel.

Victory is yours, and mine says the Lord. When we allow the Holy Spirit to be operative in our lives we are opening ourselves up to God's infinite blessings. Our Heavenly Father is the source of love and strength. Jesus wants us to recognize that all we have to do is ask. In God we can depend upon. His word says:

> "You may ask me for anything in my name, and I will do it"
>
> John 14:14

There's a song with the lyrics: "I am everything I am because you love me." Jesus loves and cares for us. My bible tells me so. Today and all my tomorrows, I will choose to believe in the best outcomes. Remember your faith as mustard seeds today and have a wonderful day!

FOR LOVE'S SAKE

"Love and faithfulness meet together; righteousness
and peace kiss each other. Faithfulness springs forth
from the earth, and righteousness looks down from
heaven. The LORD will indeed give what is good, and
our land will yield its harvest"

Psalm 85:10–12

L et me ask you: Have you ever heard the term a "righteous
love?" Well, everything was righteous in the 60's and 70's,
the hair, clothes, car, whatever you wanted to say was cool.

As a teenager, I remember hearing the cliché, "Man that suit
is righteous!" Now many of those same fashions have returned.
This term was adopted during a time when roller skates had four
wheels with ball bearings and if the skates were worn out, skate-
boards were created from them. This was a time when we actually
listened and danced to 45's and 33's. Now this era is known as
"Old School." The Motown charts were soaring; Afro puffs, and
bell-bottoms and all-star sneakers were the dress code. When
music was not "sampled" (some young musicians use other artists' music) and lyrics to songs were just suggestive, not explicit.
When groups that wore identical clothing and sang of a righteous deep love, sang love songs.

There are now radio stations that are formatted to play Old
School music exclusively. There are those of us who will forever
love Old School. This Old School music makes me wonder if in
our search for love, would we recognize it? Does the music really
convey the height, depth and real meaning of love? Was it something contrived by poets and movie directors who never knew

quite how to convey righteous love and what it resembles? Paul in the book of Ephesians prays that all saints will:

> "…know this love that surpasses knowledge—that you may be filled to the measure of all the fullness of God. Now to him who is able to do immeasurably more than all we ask or imagine, according to his power that is at work within us."
>
> Ephesians 3:19–20

It seems that the more grown up I become, the more I realize that there's so much to experience about God's love. Our brand of conditional love for ourselves, each other and our loved ones cannot possibly sustain us. But God's love certainly can. If we allow it, God's love can minister to all of our life's circumstances. It will lift you up right out of your deepest despair! Have you connected with that power source that will keep your heart and mind? My love alone is not equipped to handle day-to-day complexities. My husband will say to me sometimes, "I'll be glad when love comes and sees about me." Often in our journeys, we are left feeling isolated, perplexed, and unloved. Let us take on the heart of God and believe that loved ones are not intentionally neglecting to demonstrate love.

Should you find yourselves in need of a righteous love, let me suggest that you do not go searching for some old school records; but, instead do as the songwriter and singer, Donnie McClurkin suggested in "Speak to My Heart." This song reminds us to ask the Holy Spirit to do just that. Donnie's lyrics are so inspiring. Simply ask God. Our Heavenly Father will speak a clear message of love to lift our hearts out of despair.

Keep talking to me, Speak to my heart Lord Give me the words that will bring me new life. Words on the wing of the morning, the

dark night will fade away (If you) speak to my heart now. Speak to
my heart Lord.

Yes, yes that's it! God expressed his ultimate love for each of us. Our Heavenly Father shared a righteous love when he sent Jesus our way. Friends, hold on for the divine love's sake. While we are working out our love, God promises to help us when we walk through deep waters.

May you have all of God's perfect love this morning. Bless you.

GOD OUR REFUGE
AND STRENGTH

"The Lord Almighty is with us; the God of Jacob is
our fortress"

Psalm 46:11

This morning I awoke with the news on my mind of the battle in the Middle East over land, religion, and who has the right to occupy which land. Before rushing out of the door, I read *A Letter from God*. Yes, I did. It's a devotional of letters written to the reader from God. The letters are written to the reader and are signed from God. The reader is given the feeling as though God has written him a personal letter. This small pocket bound devotional was purchased as a birthday present for my adopted son, Keem. I thought it would be a wonderful reminder that God loves him; He could also be encouraged daily with scriptures written beautifully in the form of hand written words from God. I retrieved it from my stepdaughter's room, where it laid on the floor. Ironically enough, the letter I read was for a time of distress. How appropriate.

Seldom do I watch Night Line or any other news programming before I go to bed. Often that's too disturbing and I don't want to have nightmares. Yesterday evening was an exception to the rule. The news topic was dealing with the crisis in the Middle East. The bloody battle between the Israelis and Palestinians continues escalating. We are bombarded with this news daily. So, this morning the war and its effect seemed to be on my mind. My favorite radio personality, Tom Joyner, must have also been concerned with the devastation of the war. He interviewed a prominent pastor who also discussed this bloody battle. His concluding comment advised that we should pray, especially with battle tanks now in Bethlehem; a resolution of the crisis was imperatively necessary.

When I reached my desk, instead of opening my scripture, I was drawn to the computer. I found the CNN web site and actually viewed the pictures of the Middle East struggle. Militia, tankers, dead bodies, funerals, collapsed walls, and carnage right in my work cubical. It was up close and personal. It was plain as day that the suffering of both the Israelis and the Palestinians was reaching record proportions. I have had enough of the bloodshed and visible heartache. I obviously was distracted; my focus was off. I needed to spend time with our Father before I tackled my workload. I opened my bible and the Lord would have it that I would go directly to the passage:

> God is our refuge and strength, An ever-present help in trouble, Therefore we will not fear, though the earth gives way. And the mountains fall into the heart of the sea, Though its waters roar and foam and the mountains quake with their surging. There is a river whose streams make glad the City of God, The Holy place where the Most High dwells. God is within her; she will not fall; God will help her at the break of day.
>
> Psalm 46:1–5

I believe the Lord is conveying to His people that although pain and suffering are going on, we can trust God in all of our circumstances. One of my favorite gospel artists, Donnie McClurkin, sings about just that. Donnie asks a pointed question, as you listen to the song, you realize its Jesus asking you the questions.

Can you trust God in all of your circumstances? What is

your hurt? What if it doesn't work the first time and you call my name and don't feel me near? Will you dare believe in me? What a powerful song. Like Donnie, our response should be:

"I will trust, No matter how hard in my troubled times. In my sadness, In all my hurt Everyday, everyday I will trust you. Yes I will. Yes I will!"

During your drive home, should you happen to turn your radio on and hear the news reports, don't become distracted; hold on to your faith in our Lord and Savior Jesus Christ. Let's continue to pray for the world. God is our refuge and strength.

Be blessed in you're going out and coming in.

HOLY LIVING

"…You must distinguish between the holy and the common, between the unclean and the clean."

Leviticus 10:10

This morning there was a full blown battle. *It was on!* That's how the young people describe confusion, an outbreak. You know, a rumble! The Spiritual World Wrestling Federation stopped by my house this morning—not a soul informed me this was going on. There was obviously some spiritual warfare brewing and I was totally oblivious to it.

It started with my son; I called his name and then reminded him to get moving so he'd be on time for a field trip. Mind you this is my precious son who barked back a less than loving answer. I then noticed that my stepdaughter was seated at the computer playing solitaire. I instructed her to go take a shower while the bathroom was free. She also gave me a tone of voice that said… *I'll move when I'm ready.* I spoke to her twice.

Then I returned to my closet to select a work uniform. The voice I heard inside my head was so audible. It was so clear I can still hear…*I bet she hasn't moved.* You know you spoke to her and she just took her sweet time yesterday and rolled her eyes at you." Before that voice had become inaudible, I was standing in my door speaking like a woman I did not recognize.

My husband, in his most calm voice, stated I was growling. My tirade did not stop. I continued saying that we couldn't think twice about being disrespectful to our folks; they'd snatch our vocal cords out. I marched down the stairs only to be overtaken by garbage bags and a sink with dirty dishes. I didn't mention food that the children had left open and out on the countertop.

God was up to something. This was a test and I was failing miserably. In the ride to work I placed my hand in my husbands. He said oh so sweetly, "You realize that this is all spiritual." That's not the answer I needed. It was the truth. Everyone in my house appeared to be himself or herself; there were no facial changes or anything unrecognizable about them. My sacred ground had become a boxing ring of self-will vs. determination. Do you know the scripture that says we fight not against flesh and blood, but spiritual wickedness? See for yourself. It's in Ephesians. Let me give you a hint. The operative word is "wrestle." Check out your concordance.

My husband teased me that I was trying to repent with the handholding; probably, but, I needed assurance and said that I never wanted to speak unkindly, but had enough of the open defiance and disrespect. I came to my desk feeling like it was the wrong start for my day. I picked up my devotional and read from my Joy for the Journey devotional. I read what first appeared; a devotional focused on finding joy in the workplace. I wondered what that had to do with the morning's malaise. My joy factor was now gone.

Then I read from the scriptures:

> "Whatever you do, work at it with all your heart, as working for the Lord, not for men…"
>
> Colossians 3:23

I thought, *okay Lord.* But I just couldn't get past my morning battle of the wills. Then it occurred to me; God had set me up to show me His expectations for all of us on living holy. In my bible are subtitles for scriptures. This gives one some idea about what one is about to read. The title before Colossians 3 is: "Rules for Holy Living." In this are clear instructions for how I should handle myself in my home. I was guilty as charged. The devil had slammed me in my own ring; my home was his wrestling match and he had clearly gotten the upper hand. He whispered in my ear (it was quite audible) and my outburst spoke for itself. Peace had gone out the door. I had not…

> "…rid (myself) yourselves of all such things as these: anger, rage, malice, slander, and filthy language from your lips."
>
> Col. 3:8

The bible clearly says that I must:

> "…put on the new self, which is being renewed in knowledge in the image of its Creator."
>
> Col. 3:10

This morning I said…*forgive me, Lord, for falling for the devil's okie-dokie.* Does it happen in your household? Does holy living get tossed to the side some mornings—let's not talk about some days? Our instructions are clear. The Lord has set the mandate.

> "Therefore, as God's chosen people, holy and dearly loved, clothe yourselves with compassion, kindness, humility, gentleness and patience. Bear with each other and forgive whatever grievances you may have against one another. Forgive as the Lord forgave you. And over all these virtues put on love, which binds them all together in perfect unity."
>
> Col. 3:12–14

At 5:30 p.m., I must go home and restart my day with an apology for my display; and love my family for correction. I plan to Live Holy.

May God bless and keep you.

The Abrupt Move
of God's Healing

"Because you have made the Lord, who is my refuge, even the Most High, your dwelling place, no evil
shall befall you, nor shall any plague come near your
dwelling."

Psalm 91:9–10

C an you believe I was looking forward to seeing my own
family physician? I had enough of the group doctors' visits.
No more explaining the same information with another unfamiliar physician each time I needed medical attention. I would later
learn that my new physician and I had several similar attributes.
We are the same age and race. Our health risk indicators cannot
be overlooked. This woman shared so much information today,
that I am convinced she is knowledgeable beyond her years. She
is petite in stature, but unafraid to hit you where it hurts. Her eye
contact is intense and does not blink when she speaks. Old folks
might say, "Baby, she ain't got much of a bedside manner." Today,
I felt the urgency to take heed and not deny any of the truth. Her
abrupt manner didn't disturb me; I sensed she was sharing information that was for my good.

I'm not quite sure how I drew this parallel, it seems to stand
out for me that our relocating to Virginia is much like my new
physician's behavior; abrupt. I believe God is teaching me something, once again.

Once we relocated to Virginia, our familiar world came to
an abrupt halt. We had to relearn everything. I felt like I was in
kindergarten all over again. Driving short distances didn't exist

anymore. Everywhere we went was an excursion. My first job as an Adjunct Professor took me from Virginia Beach to Newport News. One of my big concerns was getting through the tunnel safely before 5 p.m. rush hour. It seemed that there were constant news reports about cars being smashed to smithereens. Walking to the store or to visit a friend was too far to even consider. Paying for utilities and keeping them on was another challenge that I wasn't accustomed to. My family and I enjoy people and are open, we had to discern well-intentioned folks, from those that just wanted to feel us out and learn what they could about whom this new family was. "No we're not military, or students, no we have not been transferred by a big company. Yes, we were prompted to move—God said, "Go!"…and we did. This perplexes many people we meet.

In the midst of all this sudden change, my anxiety level was heightened and my prayer life was soaring. I prayed that we would meet well-intentioned people. I prayed that my husband's ministry was not in vain. I prayed for a sincere physician. I prayed for the right employer. I prayed that my son would meet good and loving young people, just like him. I prayed that this move would not do me in. Financially it seemed much too much to live, more than what our dwindling bank account could stand. Spiritually, mentally and emotionally, I was in a new place. I sometimes felt like a displaced person.

How must a refugee feel? Poet, Langston Hughes wrote in a poem entitled "Refugee":

> Loneliness terrific beats on my heart, bending the bit-
> ter broken boughs of pain. Stunned by the onslaught
> that tears the sky apart I stand with unprotected head
> against the rain. Loneliness terrific turns to panic and
> to fear, I hear my footsteps on the stairs of yesteryear,
> Where are you? Oh, where are you? Once so dear.

LINDA MOSE MEADOWS

When I viewed my life from my perspective, I couldn't get past my feelings. I felt this great sense of loss and loneliness. It was a dry place. Now I choose to divert my attention and look at what God had done for me during that difficult transition; it was as though God was waiting for me to abandon my perspective and simply surrender to His will. The moment, the split second that I believed we'd drown, God would send a human angel our way. Stumbling blocks would become building blocks; doors of opportunity flung open and defeat would be abruptly halted. I recall our landlord saying, "I don't know why I'm doing this." We had numerous extensions for paying our rent. I had to abandon my refugee status of limited hope and embrace a new level of faith in God's possibilities. God proved Himself over and over again. I couldn't wallow in self-pity long. Yes, this realization was necessary, if I was to survive in my season. I then knew that God had brought us to Virginia and was with us every step of the way. My husband had heard it correctly—we were supposed to relocate when and how we did.

I continue to pray that my faith not waiver. For I know now, that in our seasons of despair God can abruptly halt the pain and move us to a new place of restoration; abrupt healing, yes that's what we can have. Without a shadow of a doubt our refugee status is only for a season.

> "There is a time for everything, and a season, for every activity under heaven: A time to be born and a time to die, A time to plant and a time to uproot, A time to kill and a time heal, A time to tear down and a time to build, A time to weep, and a time to laugh."
>
> Ecclesiastes 3:1–4

Friends, I am pleased to report that God continues to heed my prayers on every turn. Often the results have been startling, albeit, so remarkable. Think about your life and reflect on how remarkable God has been to you. Join me in embracing an abrupt change in lifestyle. Believe that this is the most important time in your life.

We, who are a part of the family of faith, must trust God completely in every area of our lives. He's our divine support system. God has directed me to a woman, a physician who chooses not to sprinkle her words with pleasantries. She has a direct approach; coddling is out of the picture. Today, I was informed that I faced several health risks and I could choose to do something or not; it's all up to me. God is just that way friend. We can choose to see and do things with our limitations or abruptly start on a spiritual plan that has all the health benefits for eternal living.

"We know also that the Son of God has come and has given us understanding, so that we may know Him who is true; and we are in Him who is true, even in His Son Jesus Christ. He is the true God and eternal life." (I John 5:20)

Walk in your power, have a good morning.

His Abiding Love

"To the Lord I cry aloud and He answers me from His Holy hill. I lie down and sleep; I awake again, because for the Lord sustains me."

Psalm 3:4,5

This morning I sat in my small windowless work cubical to tackle the assignment before me. Sometimes, attention deficiency takes over and I let it. I knew what I needed to focus on, I just wasn't quite prepared. I read a few inspirational things, walked to the lounge room; got my first cup of ice water and fought through the mindset of boredom as I made my way back to my desk.

God had a mental jolt in store for me that I was not prepared for, nor did I desire to share. Please know that I asked Jesus… *Why? Why the need to rehearse, such a painful time in my life? How will this benefit a soul?*

Wouldn't you know yesterday evening He revealed the answer? As I listened to a favorite minister's tape, there was my answer. (Hey friends the moral is don't ask God a thing if you're not ready to receive the truth.) The minister said, "God's people never want to share their struggles. We want to walk around as though we've never been through a thing. Everything we've done was on our own. That's the furthest thing from the truth." This minister further said, "God never gets the glory when we have been silent about our suffering and how God's grace helped us overcome." I then reflected that if we have the word of God deep within us, no matter the horrible circumstance, we'll know that we know, God knew all about our suffering. Here's the scripture that's the living proof:

"When you pass through the waters, I will be with you; And through the rivers, they will not sweep over you. When you walk through the fire, you will not be burned; the flames will not set you ablaze."

Isaiah 43:2

So, now I'm humbled and say, "Here I am Lord use me."

I'm sure He responded, "Okay, gladly..."

While at the computer, I was doing a committee assignment to learn what reading programs existed in this area's public schools. Certainly, this should be easy to access; I would simply visit each elementary school site on the web and presto. One of the school sites had chosen the picture of a roaring lion lying upon a bolder. I was not ready for the flood of feelings that would visit me at work. My sudden anxiety was too big for that cubicle. I had long ago buried the hurt of a disappointing first marriage. The feelings came tumbling back. My mind took me back to the Buffalo Zoo; I have a photo that my son loves looking at. I could see me standing in front of the polar bear pond. These bears were white in color, but their coats had green and blue splotches. I remember thinking that this must have been from the chlorine. My son was such a sweetie sitting in his stroller. This was another outing that he and I would enjoy with my wonderful friend, Cassandra.

Cassandra was the sister that my mother had not birthed. She was my confidante, consoler and a friend that did not mince words. If I behaved out of character she'd bring it to my attention. If I needed a shoulder to cry on she'd offer. If I needed to take back control over my life, she'd ask, "Linda, whose life is it anyway?" There I sat in my cubicle remembering a time when I thought that I had been a dutiful child, an obedient daughter, a loving mother, a graduate from two universities and old enough to know better. But my marriage was crumbling and home was not a safe haven. To escape the overwhelming loneliness and hurt I filled my days with busyness. I stayed occupied; my infant son was my traveling companion. I'd fill his diaper bag, pack goodies and a lunch, put a few dollars in my pocket for the gas tank, and throw his stroller in the trunk of the Toyota and sailing we'd go. Weekends we'd be on our adventure. Friends would comment you're never home. You name the cultural event; we'd be there. I just refused to lie down and die.

At that time I could not conceive the thought that God could be aware of my pain and also be in my presence. I was oblivious and un-accepting of this truth. Secretly, I was angry with God. In all of that discomfort, I carried a nagging hurt in my belly. I believed not a soul could detect it from my smiles and sunny disposition. Oh, but God knew. The anxiety was real. It manifested itself in my hair loss. I had plenty of thick hair, so I'd hide the dime sized bald spots, which soon grew to half dollars. My cousin was my beautician and would provide me with sage spiritual wisdom. She was a woman of God. I never said I did not believe her, but wondered if God heard her. It seemed my prayers were being ignored. The scripture says:

> "Dear friends, do not be surprised at the painful trial you are suffering, as though something strange were happening to you but rejoice that you participate in the sufferings of Christ, so that you may be overjoyed when his glory is revealed."
>
> I Peter 4:12,13

Obviously, I didn't have enough of God's word deep in me to encourage myself. I had to go outside to seek comfort. My husband at the time was unable to provide any emotional support. Suffering is a fact of life for all of us. Those of us in the body of

Christ are not exempt from pain. Rote prayers to stop the pain will not deter God's plan. As a result of suffering, I know this now. Prayers were like breathing for me. I must have asked God on countless occasions to "fix" my husband—stop the counter-productive behavior and make our life better. I ached for comfort and was hurting miserably. Never letting on to my family my personal anguish, I struggled through. My mama and Cassandra knew, they never beat me up about my choice to stay in an unloving situation, God provided these loving women as my sustaining force. I was operating on the injured mode. Spiritually I was depleted. I continued to pray for things to go my way.

Over and over, I thought certainly God must know? He knew more than I. God provided me with a resilient spirit and a determination that said if my husband was not going to be emotionally available, I would have to surround myself with loved ones who were available. Yes, that also included his family. On days when I wanted to wear my hurt like a favorite warn over coat, the Lord would provide me with an abiding love and push me in the presence of loved ones. He showered me with His love through my family and friends. God's grace got me through a heart wrenching divorce. Often feelings of failure and loneliness would come to visit me. But God's abiding love would not allow this depressed state to take residence.

Oh certainly I had hoped and prayed for reconciliation and a mature mate. That was not God's plan at the time. God filed that prayer request for another time. He must have thought she's got to be kidding. He speedily provided good men for my son. In the midst of my prayers for a loving home with two parents who could weather storms, God provided a mentor program, the YMCA and a host of male family and friends. God also fixed my disposition. Cassandra mailed me an article entitled, "Laying Down Your Weapons." This article was found in Essence magazine, it caused me to rethink everything. I had taken on a sour demeanor and was angry. The fact of the matter was, I didn't want to be another living statistic of a single black mother, raising a son. So I embraced my reality and continued to nurture and love my son. God provided me with the contentment to do that.

God is so tremendous; he answered prayers and shored up my sanity.

> "It is God who arms me with strength, And makes my way perfect."
>
> Psalm 18:32

He kept me from the wolves. My family had demonstrated and shown me love. I lived in love and knew what it looked like. I knew how to love and treasure my friends and they gave it right back. This love could only come from God. In my brokenness dwelled a strengthening power. Many years later God would answer my prayer with a husband of His own choosing, a husband who knows how to be a friend, believe in the power of prayer and live in love.

God has an abiding love for you and me. If you are now in a place of deep hurt and are perplexed on all sides, be confident that our Father knows your circumstance. Be not discouraged, God will take care of you. Just as the song writer encourages. Go on, I dare you, break out in song and believe it. Your struggle will become your testimony about our Father's abiding love.

> "He hath made everything beautiful in its time. He has also set eternity in the hearts of men; yet they can not fathom what God has done from beginning to

end. I know there is nothing better for men than to be happy and do good while they live."

Ecclesiastes 3: 11,12

Have a good morning!

Grace & Mercy

"Every good and perfect gift is from above, coming down from the Father of heavenly lights who does not change like shifting shadows"

James 1:17

Lord let me hear your voice this morning. That was my earnest petition. I had leisurely talked with several colleagues this morning and all the conversations seemed to be focused in the right direction. The night before I had intended to ask my husband if he felt I had given a colleague the correct spiritual advice regarding her relationship with her daughter. My husband concurred this morning that I had, and also suggested a specific scripture that referenced her concern directly. Another colleague and I spoke about her work in marriage ministry and her heartfelt desire to become more deeply involved in this endeavor. She had stated that her involvement with other churches in their ministry endeavors had taken her from doing this in her home church.

I suggested that possibly God had planned it that way and her involvement with other churches was part of a divine plan. I choose to believe that God had planned her steps to prepare her for this season. I navigated my way back to my desk, with ice water in hand. And now I needed to hear an encouraging word and whine on a friend's shoulder. I did just that.

Several days ago, our car stopped on a busy thoroughfare, directly across from an automotive tune up shop. This was during rush hour. I was relieved that the breakdown occurred there, but later learned the repair would take a considerable chunk of our money. This money was earmarked for rent. Deep down I know who takes care of my family, but an old familiar dreaded feeling wanted to visit. That feeling that accompanies the voice that says: *How are you going to make it?*

I needed to speak to an understanding friend. Before I could do any work, I picked up the phone and my friend was there to receive my call, she listened and said, "Is there something I can do?" Instantly, I felt better. She had done the most important thing I needed; she listened and understood my concerns. She urged me to get to work and focus on that. This would take the emphasis off my concerns.

I took heed and signed on to my computer. Before I could bypass the computer system, it required my password. I typed my password and there was my screen saver; a beautiful tropical vision of aqua blue waters, a white sandy beach and a blue sky that kisses the mountainous terrain and tree tops. Possibly it's Aruba. I don't know. It's such an inviting scene; you'd think you could climb through the screen and go directly to the chaise lounge awaiting you on the beach. It was as though I was seeing this vision for the first time. I just stared at the scene for a moment and reflected how God provides us with His grace and mercy on our most down and defeated days. By the way I also have another screen saver as well. If I set the timer and don't use the computer within the allotted time period my tranquil scene disappears. Up pops the words GRACE and MERCY. These words zig zag across the screen and act like a seesaw. One word moves and then the other, neither word is more pronounced than the other. It's as though they're in agreement. It's difficult to separate the two.

What was the lesson this morning? I asked myself. Yes, friends our Father did honor my request, in each conversation I had with my friend and colleagues.

He spoke and said, "Go to the scripture."

"For I know the plans I have for you, declares the Lord

> "plans to prosper you and not harm you, plans to give you hope and a future, Then you will call upon me and come and pray to me, and I will listen to you. You will seek me and find me, when you seek me with all your heart."

Jeremiah 29:11–13

In my heart I knew Jesus was speaking to me. I could hear Him so clearly. I began to respond silently but my spirit was loudly proclaiming the truth that I was not abandoned. Every time I thanked him, he responded with a truth:

"Thank you, Jesus."

Your steps are ordered, don't worry, I know the plans I have for you.

"Thank you, Jesus."

Call on Me. I'm your friend. I hear you and your concerns are my concerns.

"Thank you, Jesus."

I am Jesus, full of compassion. I will provide you with the GRACE and MERCY to see you through. Especially when the unexpected comes up.

"Thank you, Sweet Jesus."

It's so clear now. Don't you see? God loves us and I can't thank Him enough.

My prayer this morning is:

> *Lord, teach us to remember that you are right here, right now in the midst of our circumstances—we are not cast down and abandoned. Because of your Grace and Mercy, we can find sweet peace and rest in your love. You have ordered our steps. Amen.*

Good morning world!

Remembering God's Faithfulness

"Know therefore that the Lord your God, is God; He
is the faithful God, keeping His covenant of love to a
thousand generations of those who love Him and keep
His commands"

Deuteronomy 7:9

Probably one of the most difficult journeys I've ever taken was
my faith journey with my husband and son. This wasn't just
another intimate moment at the dinner table or a ride through
the park where we imagined what it would be like to start over.
This journey was to a place I knew nothing about. Moving to
Virginia has been more than just a physical move, but a spiritual
journey as well.

This journey has taken me to a place where God has gotten
our full attention. Sometimes this is a lonely place, a place I didn't
recognize. In Buffalo we shut down the business, packed up our
belongings; posted a "For Sale" sign in front of the house; had a
joyful farewell, and kissed our loved ones goodbye. The time had
come to be strong in our faith.

Our faith walk was now underway. Together my husband and
I embraced a new faith walk filled with God's promises. This was
a difficult time for me. My mother, Clarinda is an absolute jewel.
She has been there for me when my world was tumbling in; she
was my back up when I needed her to look out for my son and;
my mentor when I needed some spiritual guidance, of course, a
loving friend like no other. And then I fell in love with a great
man of faith, a praying man who would say what his old Pastor

Ureese Chillis would say: "Don't tell me what God won't do; tell me what you don't believe." This touched me profoundly.

> "…come, and let us go up to the mountain of the Lord, to the house of the God of Jacob. He will teach us His ways, so that we may walk in His paths."
>
> Isaiah 2:3

I am a woman of hope and want to live above mediocrity. So like the scripture implies my husband and I walked on God's path. I shared all of that with you because my mother will be celebrating her sixty-fifth birthday and I am far from her and want so much to be with her on her day, but God would have it that I am here and she is there a twelve hour drive away. What gift can I possibly give a mother who has loved unconditionally; four children and now there are grandchildren and extended family. Mama, who like me, many years ago traveled to a place with her husband and had to depend upon the hand of God. God was right there, even in her poverty and loneliness. He did not fail her. He kept His promises to her and her fore parents and the residual blessings are now mine.

Friends let me tell you my mother is blessed on so many turns. Currently she's physically suffering with debilitating arthritis, but continues to push her way through. She swims and encourages her friends to do the same. If you ever needed a loving word, she can provide that too. Every time I converse with her she lifts my spirit with loving words of encouragement. The only gift I can share with my mother is the gift she's given to me. She's demonstrated her faithfulness in God; she didn't topple over when life's disappointments came and wanted to take lodge with her. She continually assures me that when difficulties arise, "This too shall pass." I always remember God's faithfulness when I think of her, speak with her and look upon my mother's face.

On her sixty-fifth birthday, once again like when we were little kids, Mama would give us her money so we could buy the gift. Well she's done that again for me at forty-five years old. I'm continuing on this journey, and she's given me the wonderful gift of God's faithfulness. I celebrate my mother's legacy with all of you that are holding the hand of Jesus as we journey with faith in our hearts and hope in our spirits. This scripture wonderfully speaks of keeping God's covenant of love:

> "Know therefore that the Lord your God is God; He is the faithful God, keeping his covenant of love to a thousand generations of those who love him and his commands."
>
> Deuteronomy 7:9

During this faith journey, I encourage you to put your bags down for a moment and reflect on your life as you hold this scripture in your heart.

> "You saw with your own eyes the great trials, the miraculous signs and wonders, the mighty hand and outstretched arm, with which the Lord your God brought you out. The Lord your God will do the same to all peoples you now fear"
>
> Deuteronomy 7:19

Join me in saying, "Happy Birthday Mama, I love you."
May God bless and keep you.

LINDA MOSE MEADOWS

CALLED

"Here my cry, O God; listen to my prayer."

Psalm 61:1

Do you remember this? This past Sunday, in the afternoon, any glimpse of sun had gone, and a gray, rainy day was now evident. The rain was cold and came in a rushed downpour. Cool weather replaced the warm air but with this dreariness, came a delightful gift. The gift standing at our door was our friends—new friends, with a familiar old feeling of comfort. Comfort in our exchanges, comfort in our hearts and comfort in the fact that we were all at a place of acceptance. Our friends came bearing love in the form of hugs; warm embraces and arms loaded with goodies. These goodies were the blessed extension for creating a feast. Their visit was a breath of fresh air. The pleasant atmosphere was a nice change of pace from our routine Sunday afternoon! Sunday was a wind down from what felt like an extended week and a weekend that was never to come.

Saturdays feel like a blur when combined with house chores and yard work. But despite that, it was a time to reconnect with family and friends. For a change, everyone was not running to meetings, school and work obligations. All directions pointed home. It was as though we were all answering the call to assemble at home, under the same roof at the appointed hour. It felt good. The Lakers were tearing up the basketball court, the music was mellow and the baked and fried chicken smells wafted through the air. Peace had taken a seat on the sofa and wasn't in any rush to leave. It felt good to be in closed quarters.

Before our friends arrived, they called to make sure that I was in agreement with the plans for dinner. I said, "Sure come on." And I meant it. My planned menu of chicken and rice had now grown to a full-fledged feast. How blessed we were. It was sumptuous and our friends had beautifully complemented the meal. It reminded me of Jesus when he fed five thousand with two fish and five loaves (John 6: 9–10).

Friends, you realize that God does that so wonderfully—He stretches the resources to us. Think about the time He did this right before your eyes, you never expected it!

> "O Lord, You are my God; I will exalt you and will
> praise your name. For in perfect faithfulness you have
> done marvelous things, things planned long ago."
>
> Isaiah 25:1

After dinner we ended up relaxing and my friend asked me a question for which I didn't know if I had the answer or correct response. This question made me focus accordingly on my role in ministry. Never had I thought of myself in ministry, just my husband. My friend said, "Linda, I take God literally." That caused my spirit to stand at attention. She further said, "I believe when He said…"and the two shall become one. That means you married into ministry, you are also in ministry." My friend further urged me to pray and seek God's answer regarding my concerns. I knew quickly that God had sent me friends. He was speaking to me through her words of loving truth.

My dear friend was correct. This call I didn't quite grasp. My intellect and research abilities aren't required for this call. In case you were wondering, there is no desire for me to pastor a church. Nor is there a desire for me to build a Sunday skyscraper that beckons you to come in. And, I know that if I sang a solo, you would shout me down. But I do desire to share a loving word, God's word. I do desire to change a life. I do desire to give a hand

and open my heart. I do yearn to experience God every day of my life. And I now desire to totally believe God for all things and invite you into this spiritual ministry that will positively change your walk forever.

Yes, I believe that just as my friend called before arriving on my doorstep to make certain that they were invited for dinner and then provided us with most of it. Isn't that just like a God-sent gift! God does the same for all who are members of this family of faith. He beckons or calls us to his ministry of faith. When we have obediently embraced the ministry of Jesus Christ; our ministry then becomes evident to all that if He has done for the least of these, certainly I too, stand a chance to benefit from His mercy and grace.

This morning, I am confident in believing that God is saying to us to *try me, carry my ministry in your hearts and watch your life unfold before your very eyes*. Then our faith filled lives will demonstrate to all that believe—our Heavenly Father is abundantly capable. God provides the bounty of forgiveness, love, wisdom, guidance, nurturing, healing, sustenance and provision.

> "Then He said to them all: If anyone would come after me, he must deny himself, and take up his cross daily, and follow me. For whoever wants to save his life will lose it, but whoever loses his life for me will save it"
>
> Luke 9:23–24

Yes, a ministry of provision—provision for every thing we need to get us through this life and on to eternal life. Come friends. Let us answer the call and "…walk humbly with God" (Micah 6:8).

Good Morning!

HAVING AUTHORITY

"I have given you authority to trample on snakes and scorpions and to overcome all the power of the enemy; nothing will harm you. However, do not rejoice that the spirits submit to you, but rejoice that your names are written in heaven."

Luke 10:19,20

D o you ever have conversations with a friend or loved one and wonder where they're going with it? It's as though the conversations have taken on a mind of their own. The conversations have gone in a direction you just didn't anticipate. My husband and I always converse about something; it could range from today's young poets like Tupac Shakur versus the poets of yesteryear like Langston Hughes or Gwendolyn Brooks. Oh, we have a great time with it. Before I know it, we're playing the game *I know more than you.* Then one of us will yell, "Ok recite me a poem for a million bucks!" We start out great, but memory lapse kicks in. One of us ad libs, (I won't tell you who) and out comes verses never seen nor heard before, laughter is born and the game is over! Today was one of those conversations, except it began in song. During our drive into work, my husband just started singing this song, as he exited off the Independence Blvd. ramp. There was a private praise and worship session going on and I wanted in.

Just want to thank you forever, and ever. For all that you've done for me. Blessings and honor and glory, They all belong to you. Thank you Jesus for blessing me—Lord you're so worthy.

This song is from the *Praise Medley (Psalms 150)* by CeCe Winans. If you've never heard it, you must, since it will bless your soul. I looked at my husband and just smiled. I absolutely love this medley. Our beloved friend, Adrian sang this during our wedding. At that moment we actually kissed heaven. The worship experience was tremendous.

As we zoomed on the highway, we began to earnestly talk. My husband said, "Girl you're getting free." I appreciated that statement. I knew what he meant, but I wanted to be sure I understood it fully. I then commented that God was truly a marvel and how I appreciated what He was doing with the devotionals. Then I asked my husband, "Does it bother you when people get in the way, trying to hinder God's progress?" I needed to know his perspective, because it nags at my peace. I was addressing all of it—the ministry, worship, and life's stumbling blocks, hurts and the continuous day-to-day hurdles. He looked at me and smiled. During disappointing and difficult times, he often just stills himself and a song wells up in his spirit. He said, "Oh it's so sweet, it's like a faint whisper and I know freedom is close."

Friends, I'll be glad when I reach that spiritual plateau. On some days, I am a little closer to the summit than others. Those are days when my spirit has raised the white flag and conceded, *Holy Ghost, please come on in, and you take over. You always handle things better than I do.*

Are you like me, in the process of becoming who God desires you to be? It's time to get this—that the spirit of hindrances and annoyances can achieve just what they've set out to do and that is to rob us of our authority. If we aren't mindful that we are of a holy nation, called, a royal priesthood, go to your bible concordance, it's all there. God awaits you.

This morning let's pray:

Lord please encourage us during those moments of defeat. Forgive us if we give over our authority to the enemy and forget to call on you Jesus. Yes, we will be still in our spirit and know you are God. Restore us, Heavenly Father with boldness and authority to fight this spiritual battle. Restore our hope. We now reclaim your peace and our thinking is reformed. We are brand new! Thank You for the renewing of our spirit, We've got the power! There is boldness in you, Jesus. And you will bring what we need. Amen.

> "Ask and it will be given to you, seek and you will find: knock and the door will be opened to you. For everyone who asks receives; he who seeks finds; and to him who knocks, the door will be opened."
>
> Luke 11: 9,10

The enemy is on assignment to steal your birthright, and if we are not careful we'll hand it over willingly. Jesus is our role model. Satan came to hinder him on countless occasions and strip his authority. Jesus might have felt betrayed, hungry, exhausted, and forsaken, but never was He defeated.

Good Morning!

New Focus/
A New Outlook

"Martha, Martha the Lord answered, you are worried and upset about many things, but only one thing is better. Mary has chosen what is better and it will not be taken away from her."

Luke 10: 41, 42

Have you ever started out your day's work with the thought of going home? It's as though this thought has taken a military presence and is standing in front and center of your mind? I know you are thinking: *What is the matter with her?* But frankly, there are many of those days and moments. Recently, I discovered I was not alone.

In the break room, I sat surrounded by my favorite colleagues. We enjoyed our lunch, shared our concerns and forecasted the afternoon's workload. With all of our political commentary, an eavesdropper would have thought that we had cabinet positions in the White House—the world's problems had been solved. For a moment there was complete silence, my friend looked over at me and said, "Well lunch is over now; I'll be going home." It was as though she was reading my mind. Laughter burst forth. Tears came to my eyes. I'm surprised that the window did not shatter.

Our minds often tell us that e*nough is enough; get your bags and let's go home. Come on beat the traffic before it gets crazy. Never mind the spreadsheets, the stale coffee, over extended meetings, and the non-stimulating dialogues. Let's move on.* This is what our senses are experiencing on a daily basis. Unfortunately much of what fills a work day is time spent doing tasks that take from the pleasure of a promising productive work experience. Busy work can deplete a productive spirit. Think about it, for those of us requiring a new focus, a new outlook—being consumed with going home to do more work is self-defeating. Ok I agree, it's time to greet the day with a positive outlook—yes, the day is eight hours, but there's so much good that can come out of our work.

My friend stated with such candor: "Linda, if I do go home, put on some comfy pajamas and enjoy the outdoor view, I'm liable to see a smudge on the window and start cleaning!"

Presto! She did it again. I said, "Exactly, we cannot sit still because we're always looking around for what needs to be done."

I am so guilty of that activity. The moment my feet hit the doorstep, I am straightening up whatever snatches up my attention first. Off I go in a whirlwind, wiping counters, commenting about the kitchen floor, picking up articles, hurling questions such as "Why is the sink filled with dishes? Who left their socks on the floor? Who placed that on the kitchen table?" No, of course it doesn't stop there. I begin tossing clothes in the washer, barely greeting my loved ones and looking at them. Never stopping to think, to really embrace them and look in their eyes with a warm "Hello, I am so glad to see you today." There was no deep breathing, no work debriefing, my work dance has now been extended into the evening and I never stopped to have a new focus. Never stopping to hear and see with new eyes what was occurring with my loved ones.

If we slow down long enough to be still, our spirits would also slow down. Before we realize it deep reflection and peace have come to visit us. Prayer might have an opportunity to be birthed out of the sweet silence and what do you know, Thanksgiving transpires. Ah, joy; yes joy; replaces anxiety and fear.

I believe that because you know the love of Christ, Jesus comes to take a seat in your heart. He simply abides there. Love now is a resident, not just there for a short visit. A new view will birth a new fellowship with a Holy Presence. As Jackie McCullough might say, "Come on and see!"

God steps in and does a mighty cleansing and for a while the problems of our world are no longer pronounced—they belong to the world and not us!

Please take a moment and *read the Holy Scripture, the book of Luke, Chapter* 10. Once you've read through to verse 41 replace your name with Martha's. I just thought about this. The Holy Spirit has instructed me to share this exercise with you, my friend. Instead of Martha, say your name out loud, so you can hear it spoken.

"Linda, Linda," the Lord answered, "You are worried and upset about many things, but only one thing is better." Like Mary choose the spiritual goal, and it will not be taken away from you. Luke 10:41,42: Jesus has done it again friends; He has something of value to say to us. Something that's only meant for our eyes and ears. Thank you Father.

I believe Jesus is saying to each of us, "Get a new focus, a new outlook on your life. Focus on me, instead of you tackling the problem." I am sure you are much like me, in that we are guilty of missing out on powerful moments spent with Jesus—distracted with thoughts, activities and concerns that push opportunities for divine fellowship in the wash cycles, trash bins, filing cabinets, and clothesbaskets of our lives.

Come on and sing with me in this medley of songs with Cee Cee Winans (Yes, I listen to her while at work): *"Power, power— wonder working power in the precious blood of the Lamb. Lamb of God, sweet Lamb of God, Wash me in this precious blood. Jesus Christ, the Lamb of God, I was so lost I should have died You have brought me to your side. Lamb of God, Holy, Holy, Holy Lamb of God, Wash me in this precious blood…"*

I am closing now and like Jesus, I want to be inclusive. I trust that you too will accept a new view—that is a spiritual view, a new outlook that takes us out of ourselves—a new radical, changing view that our Heavenly Father has of all of our wonder filled today's and all of our tomorrows.

Please join me in prayer:

- *Lord help us to be still and hear from You. When we have the opportunity, help us to see past messy desk drawers, cluttered file cabinets and demanding workloads.*
- *Lord help us to see our loved ones, loving faces over dirty dishes and overflowing clothes hampers.*
- *Lord help us to see the order of your plan over all our personal clutter and when we can't see, we'll confidently know your love is enough.*
- *Lord help us to hear you over all the noises that purposely distract us.*
- *Lord help us to marvel in your presence at work, play and at home.*
- *In the ordinary tasks, and business of the day Lord help us to have a view of you!*
- *Lord help us. We'll continue to give you all glory and honor and praise. Amen.*

Have a good day!

SOME RIGHT GOOD LOVE
A.K.A. PEARLS OF WISDOM

"The entire law is summoned up in a single command:
Love your neighbor as yourself."

Galatians 5:14

O n this Sunday morning my family would find themselves
eager to begin our hour and a half journey from Norfolk
to Drewryville, VA. This journey had the distinct feel of Sundays
that I traveled with my grandparents from Washington, D.C. to
Rockville, Maryland. Those memorable Sundays were filled with
good smells in the kitchen. Grandpop would rise early and prepare
a breakfast complete with fried potatoes and onions, scrambled
eggs, country sausage, and fried apples with cinnamon. Let me
not forget the biscuits. This hearty breakfast would carry us over
through church service, and on to a late supper. Our destination
was to get to the family church, followed by a visit to the "home
place" to see my great grandfather, Papa Brown, have dinner with
him and extended family and then return to Washington, D.C.
in the evening.

No! Today we weren't headed *up the country* (this is my
Grandpop's expression) but it surely felt like it. This Sunday,
although I awoke earlier than usual for our journey, my physical
momentum was off. I had prepared the night before, with ironing
my dress, selecting the shoes and the other essentials. I knew the
morning drill, because lately I am the last to fall in line. It never
fails; everyone is outside, much to my amazement. My son's routine is so predictable: he knocks on my door; checks on my progress at least three times; and on the fourth attempt he'll announce,

Mom we're waiting for you. I try hard not to be irritated, because I do believe that I am moving as fast as I can. My movements are obviously more deliberate and paced. Unfortunately, I didn't have time to sit and enjoy my Sunday breakfast, maybe next week.

My husband had planned the night before to leave home at 8:00 a.m. He was expected to assist with the baptism and provide the sermon. He had gotten an early start, made breakfast and was ready to move. I hurriedly dumped my cold scrambled eggs with cheese in a plastic container, topped it off with a half jelly donut and to eat my breakfast in the car. I needed a cup of water or juice, but kept that thought to myself. The cold breakfast was quite tasty and I was grateful. Although we left at the planned time, ten minutes later we were back at our door because my husband had forgotten to take his medicine. He asked me if I had taken mine and I proudly announced, "Yes while I was rushing I remembered to take mine, oh, and Mike, grab mom a glass of water while you're in the house."

"Thank you, sweetie."

"Touché!"

During the preceding weeks my husband would enjoy speaking with a kind, elderly gentleman who was the chairman of his board of deacons. There, he stood in the church door, smiling and said, "You must be Reverend Meadows?" He recognized my husband's voice. They shook hands and the formal introductions began. I decided not to follow my husband in the Pastor's office and instead went directly to the sanctuary. I felt prompted to go in that direction. God was preparing me. Sunday school was commencing. I must tell you, that there are too many Sundays when I am not present in Sunday School and today was a clear indication that I had cheated myself out of countless occasions to receive *some right good love.* I'll explain shortly.

> "This is love: not that we loved God, but that he loved us and sent his Son as an atoning sacrifice for our sins."
>
> I John 4:10

My son and I found seats next to the attendees of the class. The gentle man teaching the class obviously loved reading his bible; he zealously recited scriptures that he wove into his explanations. He openly displayed his comfort in teaching the lesson and engaging anyone that chose to dialogue with him. I sat quietly and made mental notes of scriptures that I would later read for clarity. The lesson focused on Freedom in Jesus. The class participated in reading *Galatians* 5, reviewing the outline and discussion of the text. For a moment I was a student again, soaking in all the pearls of wisdom from this engaging and enthusiastic instructor. I forgot how wonderful it felt to learn something new and hear words that would reinforce my faith. I felt as though I were a student in college again, and wisdom was speaking so I need not interrupt, because I knew what I knew, but I did not know what this man of God had burning in his heart, I listened intently.

> "But when he, the Spirit of truth, comes, he will guide you into all truth. He will not speak on his own; he will speak only what he hears, and he will tell you what is yet to come He will bring glory to me by taking from what is mine and making it known to you."
>
> John 16:13

Surely, there were pearls of wisdom that I wanted to catch that I could possibly refer to during the lean times of hectic weeks ahead. So I listened to the teacher shared what finding Freedom in Jesus meant. The instructor reminded the class that Jesus would step in at the appointed times and fight your battles if need be. The class was encouraged to not behave like the man fighting in the street, laying his religion (the teacher called it "*liggin*") down for a while and conveniently scooping it back up. The concluding thought was that Freedom in Jesus allows us to lean on our Lord and Savior and confidently know that we are never alone in this spiritual warfare. Jesus equips us with every spiritual blessing.

Oh, my instructor spoke with confidence and reminded us, that no matter what the world hurls at us, the truth is that we are fearfully and wonderfully made. That although the scripture was used to castigate and keep us in our place, when the word said, *obey your master,* that meant God, not man. Freedom in Jesus allows us to stand on God's word and having the conviction to stick with our convictions.

This ride would take us out of our comfort zone to an unknown place. This historic family church was a place God had predestined for us to visit. These Sunday school teachers and class participants each seeded a good word into my son's soul as well as mine. Sunday school would conclude. The bell was rung and all classes assembled together. The secretary read minutes, chronicled the lessons, greeted guests, and announced the closing song. And then God said, *Linda pay attention, I want you to take note.*

Class leaders were asked to select a representative who would give highlights of the Sunday school lesson. There stood another man of God, he did not need to be prodded or stroked he walked quietly to the microphone and his words were simple and powerful. This man, small in stature referenced the text:

"Thou shall love thy neighbors as thy self"

Galatians 5:14

This class leader announced that he loved himself and wanted to treat his neighbor with that same love. This man further spoke and said, "We are all the bible that some others read." Listening to his words caused me to reflect and imagine those ancestors who could not read God's word and trusted those who could read God's word but more importantly, "All that they had to go on was the example of what a Christian said and did."

> "The kingdom of God does not come with your careful observation, nor will people say, 'Here it is' or 'There it is' because the kingdom of God is within you"
>
> Luke 17:20a-21

This class leader then said, "Often folks would read only a passage and use that passage to their advantage but, they refuse to read the bible, the preceding chapters and the following verses in its entirety." How accurate this statement was. I now understand the importance of reading the entire chapter not just a verse.

Oh, saints don't you see God was at it again. My instructor announced it during the introduction to the Sunday school lesson—the Freedom we find in Jesus is *right good love.* I knew just what both my instructors were saying. God was speaking, He is reminding us that we must live the life we love to sing and talk about. We must ask ourselves and examine ourselves for the truth.

Is your walk in-line with the bible? For so many people who don't read the bible, we are all the bible they have. Never mind the grammar, isn't that good gospel? Certainly, the life that we live can be filled with the sweet freedom that belief in our Lord and Savior, Jesus Christ provides.

"So I say to you: Ask and it will be given to you; seek and you will find; knock and the door will be opened to you. For everyone who asks receives; he who seeks finds; and to him who knocks, the door will be opened"

Luke 11:9–10

March on saints, be encouraged and have a blessed day!

God's Clear
Instructions

"I rejoice in following your statues as one rejoices in great riches. I meditate on your precepts and consider your ways. I delight in your decrees; I will not neglect your word"

Psalm 119:14–16

As I stood in the quiet hall corridor outside my work location, I watched the photocopy machine push the paper out a sheet at a time—at lightening speed. I had been tediously updating a manual for quite sometime. I confess this task is one of the least stimulating. I intermittently sandwich-in other tasks while attempting to complete this project. Some of the things kindly pull me away from this tedium; which was consulting the web, updating my database, phoning other department heads, reformatting documents and rounding up walking partners for my pre-lunch hike around the corner. Yes indeed this task of updating a manual makes for long afternoons. But, so be it—someone must do it—and I am that someone.

While a section of the manual was photocopying, I glanced over my shoulder and noticed the putty colored metal file cabinet. It is filled to the brim with new and dated contracts, titles, amended documents and who knows what else. A not-so-instructive oak-colored bookcase has been stationed next to the cabinet. Your observation was correct; an office decorator had not been hired to enhance this workspace. Placed on the top shelf of this furniture were several manuals. It was apparent that no one had consulted them in quite some time. My curiosity had gotten the best of me as I thumbed through the long forgotten manuals. Many work hours had gone into selecting the entries of the narratives, graphs, flowcharts, philosophical sayings, and collected data. There were several manuals with eye-catching colors that appeared as though they were just off the press. Those pages were crisp and white. Possibly this was an extra and all department heads had been presented with their official copy for their respective units. In another three ring binder was information regarding other related agency sites, contact persons, and phone numbers. This binder had received a good workout, the papers were yellow with age and the corners of the worn pages were crinkled and folded. It would be unfair to say or imply that these instructive manuals were created, placed on a shelf for later use and then ultimately ignored. But the fact remains that there they sat, untouched and dusty.

In all of our work locations and my past experiences there are excessive sheets, binders, folders and bulletin boards filled with instructions and directives related to our vocations. Many of these papers begin to blend in with the wall coloring. If new materials are posted, it becomes lost in the layers.

These comprehensive manuals are cumbersome to carry and much too incomprehensible to read in one given day. These massive volumes are full of innovative plans and ideas for change. Have you found that the recommended change and adoption of these plans is equally elaborate as the manuals? Strategizing becomes the name of the game. Whispers, closed-door strategy meetings and management's hurried pace are a dead give away that change is surely on the horizon. Before the campaign starts, or the directive hits the bulletin board, the office is buzzing. Oh it takes a great deal of effort to ignite change even though the mandate is clear. Management understands that and consequently spends a great deal of time with elaborate plans, group discussions with set agendas, and kickoffs to spark employee excitement. Manuals help us to buy into a required plan of action.

Unfortunately, if plans and rules are not written, we don't have to accept them. Many of us resist instructions, are uncomfortable with change unless we believe there's a benefit to be gained or understand the consequences. We'd prefer to go about our routines undisturbed, accept and/or shelve or table the binder for another time.

If we are honest even as Christians, we are much the same way. Seldom do we deviate from a behavior, lifestyle or action unless we feel persuaded to change. Our Holy manuals, our Bibles, are God's clear instructions for navigating this difficult and uncertain life. Often our Bibles are placed on shelves, coffee tables, underneath the beds, on night stands and yes, in bathrooms. They are in close proximity but often untouched.

Jesus convinces us on every turn. In studying the scripture, we are tugged, pulled and spiritually pushed out of our familiar comfort zones to a new place. So many of us like to coin the phrase *God is taking us to a new level.* Well if that's indeed the truth, our new level has clear instructions, for: new living, for new behaving, for new loving, for new faith building, for continuous, new forgiving, and adopting a new life in Christ.

What is our Heavenly Father urging us to do? Oh I see it so clearly now, while I was fighting my tedium. He said:

> "...Hear, O Israel, the decrees and laws I declare in your hearing today. Learn them and be sure to follow them"
>
> Deuteronomy 5:1

Have a good morning friends!

MORE THAN ENOUGH

"The grass withereth, the flower fadeth: but the word
of our God shall stand forever"

Isaiah 40:8

Today was a leisurely Friday, a mental health day; you know a
no-workday. Several friends from work had invited me to go
with them to the "Pottery." Someone planted the seed of taking a
Friday off and doing something fun outside of work. I was game.
I am no longer big on shopping and malls are my least exciting
place to be. I am not quite sure when that came about, but I am
learning that I really do have more than enough. As I approach
forty-five years old, I now understand what folks mean when they
insinuate that they have *enough stuff*.

My friends walked around work as though we were planning
some great espionage. You can't convince me that someone outside this circle was not aware. Nevertheless it was fun, anticipating what the day's find at the Pottery would bring. So Thursday
came and we spoke in code, planned our points of departure and
snickered about the anticipated shopping good time that lay
ahead. I've only visited the Pottery once, but it was a memorable
trip. I had twenty dollars to splurge. My husband and I walked
around the Pottery; and enjoyed the wonderful yard treasures, art
and plants. But I looked up and read a sign outside the Oneida
Outlet which read: *"All dishes* $1.00." Certainly they could not
have been referring to the dishes that were stacked on the ground.
They were beautiful. I had only walked past them three hours ago
and admired them from a safe distance. I had made up my mind
that they were out of my wallets reach. I looked at the sign, then
at my husband. I inquired about the sign, and the next moment I

was bursting through the door with a shopping cart, cooing and awing over the Oneida smartly designed dishes. My treasure had been discovered. I purchased a setting for six and smiled all the way back to Buffalo.

Well this Friday in August produced no trip to the Pottery. Would you believe that three of us discovered we had car problems? So, instead of digging through dishes at the Pottery I enjoyed a wonderful breakfast, siesta and wrote this devotional at my pace. The birds were chirping, the trees swayed, and I enjoyed the breeze that flowed through my windows. I sat in my vanity chair, which once belonged to my husband's grandmother and took a look around my room. I saw shoes, not one pair, many. I then looked at my bookcase; it overflowed with journals, novels, bibles, and devotionals—all the things I treasured.

I looked at my walls with all the art hung and it radiated some significance. This art was purchased when I visited festivals, galleries and the island of Jamaica. Jamaica was a trip with friends, who were like my sisters and we ate the native dishes, walked the narrow roads and experienced the life. My observational survey went on and on. My dresser was overflowing with family photos and keepsakes.

I closed my eyes and began praying out loud, spontaneously, thanking God for all that he continues to provide. There was more than enough of everything when I was honest. Our home not only has the material things and family keepsakes that I treasure, but it has the love of family. I appreciate that my bounty includes a loving husband, who is a man of God, caring stepchildren and a child that is obedient and having a host of loved ones and extended family members. Yes there is more than enough. My cup "runneth" over with more than enough love to share and receive.

Oh friends, are you also guilty of desiring more stuff? I love dolls, scented candles (which I seldom light), family photos, keepsakes, art, shoes, dishes, and baskets. Truthfully God has blessed me tremendously and if I never make it to another flea market, pottery outlet or T. J. Maxx, I've got more than enough.

I thank God that he has blessed me to be surrounded with the comforts of home. But I do understand that the comforts of home are simply temporary things, which can be gone instantly through theft, fire and/or a disaster.

This morning I heard God clearly saying to all of us, *you've got more than enough when you have me.* We can joyfully embrace the picture; the divine picture of what really matters most in life. What matters most in life is that God will keep us in our distress, in our joy, in our peace, in our loneliness and in our hope.

> "God, who has called you into fellowship with his Son Jesus Christ our Lord, is faithful"
>
> I Corinthians 1:9

The Holy Scripture assures us that we have more than enough in Christ Jesus. We have the love of a wonderful, forgiving, all knowing, powerful, omnipotent, omniscient and omnipresent Father. When the dust settles on the dishes, the keepsakes get scattered to the four corners of the world, the shoes are worn out and the art no longer has any significance, the word of God remains.

> "Know therefore that the Lord your God is God; he is the faithful God, keeping his covenant of love to a thousand generations of those who love him and keep his commands"
>
> Deuteronomy 7:9

Have an abundant day!

Obvious Power

"He will bring glory to me by taking from what is mine and making it known to you"

John 16:14

I was itching to write this morning. Yesterday had consumed much of my time working on a project that required me to review a proposal, pull information together and then format the information in order to begin responding intelligently to a written proposal. Now I must fill in the blanks with the missing information. I had prayed before I endeavored to do the project; and yes it just began to flow. God had allowed me to create a template, an outline and then the anxiousness about my work began to ease. I thanked God that at the end of the day, there was some visible evidence for a days work. Sometimes it's not that obvious. The template actually gave me some breathing room to focus. So I rushed to my desk believing that I would get a clear word from God this morning. And wouldn't you know it, two of my colleagues were complaining about their husbands and boyfriends.

Their conversations were too overbearing to ignore. One young woman wanted and planned to see a friend from college. I could hear the excitement in her voice; she was looking forward to being with her friend. Her boyfriend was at a standstill, he wasn't sure if he wanted to go. He was undecided and time was of the essence. He needed to make a decision about going or not and either buy a train ticket at the discounted price or lose out. She said, "I'll go; he knows I've done it before!"

My mind quickly zoomed in; this was all too familiar. I recognized what I was hearing. Soon I'd be feeling that nervousness in the stomach. An argument before you could appreciate the gift of the day. This was deep hurt, but on the surface; it appeared benign. This conversation between two women could not be taken lightly. It was about their feelings; they were being disrespected, treated in an unloving manner, overlooked and quietly ignored. They danced around the issue of wanting not to be taken for granted. This morning my intentions were not to go wading in murky waters of discontent. In my own past failed marriage, those feelings were just the tip of the iceberg. There were days, months and then years of my silently battling for love and it would erupt. Erupt into ugly behaviors I did not recognize, and buried hurts and even hate when I felt that he was not giving me the deserved respect, recognition, conviction or affirmation and peace of mind I so wanted. No Lord! Not this morning did I want to stand around and join in such an arduous discussion? I did not want my feelings exposed, like laundry hanging on a line. That was too many years ago, feeling like yesterday!

I needed to hear no more because I knew that the premise of their discussion was that they felt their loved ones ignored them; didn't hear them, and then accused them of nagging. This familiar diversion—their conversation was a great technique to steer me away from what I needed to be doing—my work. I felt compelled to join the discussion, I remembered all to well in my first marriage–the struggles to communicate my feelings and then being accused of nagging when I stirred the waters and spoke up, expressed myself. Those that don't want to face problems know that focusing on the nagging moves you away from the real issues.

I could sense from their frustrated tones that invariably the miscommunication always escalated into an unpleasant verbal confrontation. Oh yes a fight would surely erupt. Doors would slam, all productive forms of communication would cease and the war of wishes would be the headline for the day. The battle would be on! *Enemies take your opposite places, and may the best one win!* My soul mused and said, *No Satan, not today, I have no desire to referee.* My colleagues were intent on drawing me in, but I really wasn't interested in counseling or reliving the homeland wars. For a moment, I remembered what it felt like to hear and speak nasty accusations and then live in a stifling unloving world and operate on hurt. I know God's love can't reign there. How could I share a good word with my colleagues and not get drawn into that hurt just by the conversation? There are some reunions I no longer desire.

I removed myself from that scenario and remarked that it sounded like communication was a problem. Yeah! I know that was obvious. They concurred; one person piped up and said, "Yes, I know I am going to have to do something different." Well that was really the essence of it all. I marched to the ladies room, combed my hair and up popped the Stormie Ormon's book. Yes, that's right she has written a book entitled, *The Power of a Praying Wife.* During that brief moment alone the Holy Spirit had planted that thought. The old me hated the confrontations, and yes those episodes were ugly. But now friend, in my possession are wonderful books that a friend loaned me. Yes, they are Stormie's books. Actually, she's written several that speak about the power of praying.

The new Linda now stood before a mirror and began to reflect how some sixteen years ago, I had been so hurt by my husband whom I loved and trusted. I was determined to stay in a hurting relationship, and convince him to change. I now know that I had gone about it all wrong. My plans were void of the Holy Spirit. Oh! I prayed, but then pushed and fussed my way through. It was all so self-defeating, but it was a necessary process. That pain, that discomfort was part of my spiritual journey. It's hard for me to fathom that that was for my good. But it was.

These trials came to make me strong not kill him. The Holy Spirit just revealed to me that it was.

> "No, in all these things we are more than conquerors through him who loved us"
>
> Romans 8:37

I returned to my desk; opened a favorite devotional.

> "The Spirit Glorifies God"
>
> John 16:14

Went back and read the entire chapter and knew the Holy Spirit had been working with me. God had done it once more; when he revealed to me the title of Stormie Ormon's book, *The Power of a Praying Wife.* I now understood that there is power in prayer. I've seen and experienced this power in my own life. Visibly, obvious changes have occurred. Our lives, our husbands, our homes, our loved ones and our work atmospheres cannot remain the same when we earnestly pray and let the mysterious power of the Holy Spirit work. No, I did not have the power to change my first husband, it was much too much for me—but, I could have lived in a more peaceful home had I taken the approach. Yes, I did mention the book to my colleague, she laughed uncomfortably but, I looked at her and repeated the need for prayer and hoped she'll pass on to her friend the information. I'll be praying for them.

God has given all of us a wonderful resource—the divine connection to Jesus; and that's the Holy Ghost. Go and learn for yourself what the Holy Ghost can do. As my friend, Evangelist Wilma Taylor says, "*Oh,* but it's the essence of life." Jesus has provided us with a comforter, which is life changing. This transformation is the obvious power needed for the good of all those we love and serve. Oh I'm a witness!

Good Morning!

ONLY BE CAREFUL

"Only be careful, and watch yourselves closely so that
you do not forget the things your eyes have seen or let
them slip from your heart as long as you live. Teach
them to your children and to their children after
them"

Deuteronomy 4:9

Honestly, I felt as though there was nothing more to be said. I love writing these devotionals; but, felt so undeserving these past few days. I have been stunned and bothered that I just couldn't bring myself to write a word. Yesterday I stood in my little kitchen and announced as though I was making some great decree to my family, "I haven't written in four days." My husband replied, "What are you going to do about it?" This time, there was no quick reply. In my heart, I was actually crying out, "I can't, and I don't know why I can't!" Yes, I did know. The truth was simply that I felt that if I had sat down and attempted to write during those past four days, I would not have been doing anyone a service, and certainly God would not have been in it. That is what the enemy wanted me to believe, that maybe God was no longer revealing his glory to me everyday. I was crushed.

Oh, but today brought something sweet and new. He brought a word clear and convincing. My spirit says, *Thank you Jesus.*

When I reflect on those days, it's as though they were a confusing dream. The series of events did not connect. The sequence seemed so out of order. I had been bombarded with disappointments, and I could have easily submitted to that, but I chose instead to focus and analyze all the mess that had occurred over a four-day span. It was as though confusion rang my doorbell,

LINDA MOSE MEADOWS

walked into my kitchen, got some food and made itself at home. I was consumed with the feeling I had. I was feeling out of sync, and hurt. These feelings were generated out of several uncomfortable conversations, work overload, unrealistic expectations that I had placed on myself and others. All of this felt so unproductive and I just couldn't pass go, nor collect $200. The game was on me, you couldn't convince me to let things go. The hurt appeared real, legitimate and true to form. I cried, sobbed real tears and resolved that some things were just unacceptable.

With all of that confusion, God was never inaccessible. I see it very clearly, now friends. God wanted me to only be careful. I should be careful to know that God was still God, and in control. Oh I know I've said it before, I just couldn't grasp that then. My faith had plummeted. I would like to think that possibly, I wasn't supposed to grasp that then.

Often the diversionary tactic that the enemy uses is to steal our joy. Know without a doubt that the enemy will only steal and kill your joy when you are on the brink of good. Good in your homes, good in your relationships, good in your future, and good in your souls! As my dear friend, Anna says, "He (the enemy) has peeped into your future and sees what's about to take place." So the hurt is magnified and the confusion will hit you when you least expect it. Undoubtedly, this melee will be in the midst of your comfort zone—zones where you retreat and find respite.

Then you wonder…*is there any thing safe or sacred?* Loved ones that are near and dear to your heart will become unrecognizable, because of out of character behavior. And then there's an outbreak of harsh words, character assassinations, benign neglect, blaming, finger pointing, explosions of outrageous anger; and love cowers in the corner, too bruised to battle. It is spiritual warfare at its finest and not a soul recognizes the modus operandi.

Oh, but I've come to share with you that after my spiritual

battle, I am limping back into the safe arms of our Heavenly Father. During those four days, my prayers were clips of words, lathered with confusion and heartbreak; I now know God had not forsaken me.

Our God can do exceedingly and abundantly more that you and I can possibly know. Friends, I felt as though my devotionals had come to an abrupt halt and I would just be a hypocrite, writing to inspire you and feeling defeated and dejected personally.

Like all of us I was alive with hurts that began to consume my every other thought, and disappointments harboring in my spirit. Despite all of that, there remains great hope for you and me.

This morning, yes, this morning I opened an old June/July 2000 *Our Daily Bread* and read, "Don't forget!" And then referenced Deuteronomy 4:9: "Only be careful, and watch yourselves closely so that you do not forget the things your eyes have seen or let them slip from your heart as long as you live. Teach them to your children and to their children after them." God opened up my understanding. I now understand that the discomforts of life with its unrecognizable confusion and disappointments serve a direct purpose.

What the devil meant for my demise God meant for my good…

> "Acknowledge and take to heart this day that the Lord is God in heaven above and on the earth below. There is no other."
>
> Deuteronomy 4:39

God allowed me to feel and encounter hurt, firsthand, in my home, at my dining room and breakfast table. Those are sacred places in my home. (We sit at the table and share joys, laughter and resolve family matters.) He then directed me to read what Moses reminded his people. Moses clearly said that if they'd only be careful to remember what God had done for them in the wilderness and continue to obey God's commandments, they could take possession of the land.

That scripture of *Deuteronomy* 4 provided me great affirmation. Those written words were reassuring me that I must continue in being passionate about God's word and writing even if my comfort zone is torn to shreds. God always throws us a lifeline, whether we recognize it or not.

God is giving us powerful lessons friends. We are not defeated but we must be careful to remember what God has done for us in our hurtful yesterdays, roller coaster today's, and confidently believe:

> "You were shown these things so that you might know that the Lord is God; besides him there is no other. From the heavens he made you. On earth he showed you his great fire, and you heard his words from out of the fire. Because he loved your forefathers and chose their descendants after them, he brought you out of Egypt (you select the place where God rescued you) by his Presence and his great strength, to drive out before you nations greater and stronger than you and to bring you into their land to give it to you for your inheritance, as it is today."

> Deuteronomy 4:35–38

Only be careful…Have a blessed morning!

Wake Up Call

"As for God, his way is perfect; the word of the Lord is flawless. He is a shield for all who take refuge in him"

2 Samuel 22:31

Can you imagine wanting to get to work on Monday morning? Well, this was one day that I wanted to rush to my workstation and get right to it. Actually I wanted to put out a clarion call to all my prayer partners—"Come quick and come now!" I was in need of a major distraction, mostly attention.

It's rare that I have the opportunity to sleep a little late on Monday morning. This morning, I was to return to my physician's office for a fasting blood sugar. The receptionist had made her reminder call on Friday afternoon. I got it! Explicit instructions weren't needed, I understood that after midnight on Sunday I was to eat and drink nothing until my blood sample was drawn. So this morning at 10:30a.m., I was ready for the test but, unprepared for the news. The doctor delivered her wake up call.

I've shared with you how curt and direct my physician is. She's as thorough as she is curt, moving with lightening speed. Her consultations are equally as pleasant. Once again she didn't blink when she shared my prognosis with me. Before she could utter another word, I interrupted and requested that my husband sit in the room with me. I needed him to hear what I knew I would miss. I sensed bad news. My doctor's demeanor did not change for a split second. She looked at him and then at me and pronounced, yes; I had the beginning stages of diabetes.

Do you know that I have difficulty saying diabetes? The brochures I received were equally as unsettling. The word 'Diabetes' was printed on them as big as outdoors signs. The pamphlets and brochures were glossy, clever, and attractive—real attention-grabbers. People were smiling and appeared to be happy, acceptance was written all over their faces. All I could think was, *Please, who wants to smile at this deadly thing? It's a disease!* Please understand that I really am having difficulty in sharing this. As I tried to filter through my doctor's words, tears began to stream. I couldn't cut them off. I wanted to maintain my composure and not totally lose it. Finally she left the room and my husband stood up and hugged me. He consoled me and said, "It's not as bad as you think, what else is bothering you?" I trembled and thought...*I don't want to die an early death.* Does that make sense? I haven't seen my youngest niece in her toddler stage. I want to see my son graduate from high school and college. I want to witness his children giving him a rough time with back talk. I want to travel more. I have too much to see and do. My thoughts were endless. Mascara was running, and I am sure raccoon eyes had developed. Beloved family members came to mind those who suffered through strokes, dialysis machines, needles, and home care. Dreaded SUGAR! There's nothing sweet about the thought of becoming incapacitated.

As I was riding with my husband, I became defensive and said, "I'm not eating that diabetic junk! We don't eat bad, I never have." My husband in a loving and patient tone reminded me of what we did eat and how we do prepare our meals. I dare not tell you how often we eat fried chicken and fish. He was correct, there was much room needed for improvement. I wasn't quite prepared for self-reflection. Righteous indignation was the corner in which I wanted to stand. Mentally I didn't budge. Then a feeling of confusion pushed indignation aside. I was perplexed—how am I supposed to eat? What exchanges am I supposed to make? Breads for crackers, fruits for what? The enemy was having a great time with me. He put his arms around me and squeezed me tight. We were holding each other up like two drunks.

Now, you realize the pity party had begun, but I was still stuck. I pushed my way to work, I didn't do as my husband had suggested, and I go home. Instead, I needed to be around people. I felt as though I needed some distractions, but the truth was I wanted some attention. There my folks were seated at the lunch table; perfect. I said, "No one's going for a walk?" They had done that already. Then there was my cue. Some one asked, "Are you okay?"

"No, no I'm not." I then proceeded to give a synopsis of my health verdict and doctor's behavior. I exited the lunchroom and went for a walk. I heard you shout *Bravo, great performance!*

Friends, God was not acknowledging my behavior. Just like my doctor let me cry and never offered a tissue. During my walk, He meant for me to be alone. He wanted my full attention again. There was something He wanted to convey to me. Drama was not a prerequisite for today's class. As I walked, I settled into a comfortable stride and began to notice the trees, the warmth of the sun, and the birds chirping. There was instant peace. The song, "You Are My Peace" kept coming as I passed one building and then another. Before I realized it, I was humming and singing the song to myself. Let me share some of the words with you:

"You are my peace, You are my peace, You are my peace and I worship you. You deliver my soul from the hands of the enemy my peace, my peace."

Upon my return to work, my friends—some are nurses; others know about diabetes; were ready for me. They did not entertain my pity party. After seeing them, I wanted to cry. Instead I just sat for a moment. One friend replied, "Okay, it's not a death sentence." Another retorted, "So now you know what's required.

I will be back to take a look at your diet." Another added her unsolicited advice and said, "No more pity party!"

I did not want to laugh, but did and said, "Just until 5:00 p.m. I want this to last a while." They were not accepting it and then proceeded to instruct me about my fried fish and salad for lunch. What was the matter with them? I was scolded about the breading on the fish and given several scoops of chicken salad in place of the fish. At that moment I said, "It's time to be proactive."

What I really wanted to share with you is this. I came to work, feeling truly out of sorts. Upset by the diagnosis. But in reality this was a wake up call. A call to get my health issues in line with a healthier and whole me. I am kissing forty-five years of age and am over weight. It's a fact that African American women who are like me will probably suffer some severe health problems, if they don't opt for some drastic lifestyle changes. I never thought I'd suffer from hypertension but I do. I never, ever thought diabetes would hit me and it has. I never thought I'd be overweight but I am. Friends, never mind big boned. The facts speak for themselves.

I can't possibly do what God requires spiritually and become challenged by physical infirmities.

If you too are challenged with diabetes or any other health issues, know that there are so many in this struggle with you. If we choose to bury our heads in the sand, we will suffer. God has given us the opportunity to make good out of some unwelcome news. Let's choose to become proactive and treat our living temples better. And yes, I had to be arm-wrestled—oh but He's got my full attention. How about you? If you fell into the risk category as I did, consult your physician. Maybe we'll bump into each other on the walking trails. I will focus on a better me, in my minds eye, I see me fit and have begun to work towards that end.

God gave me a perfect opportunity to get this body back in reasonable order. I thank Jesus for the wake-up call.

"But the prophet Gad said to David, Do not stay in the stronghold, Go into the land of Judah…"

1 Samuel 22:5

FAITHFUL IN EVERY WAY

"Do you not know? Have you not heard? The Lord
is the everlasting God, the Creator of the ends of the
earth. He will not grow tired or weary, and his understanding no one can fathom. He gives strength to the
weary and increases the power of the weak"

Isaiah 40:28, 29

"*Hold on, old soldier, Hold on, old soldier.*" That's what the
Mississippi Mass Choir shouted over my cassette
player. The song had gotten so good to me that I'm sure I didn't
realize that I needed to turn the volume down. *"When your way
gets dark, I know the Lord will see you through, Yes, He will, You can
make it keep the faith. Hold on, old soldier."*

The Mississippi Mass Choir was right on target. I slipped
in my cassette, adjusted the volume, and tried not to strain my
hearing and disturb any colleagues that sauntered by. God was
at his handy work again—and I was fully conscious of it. My
whirlwind weekend had come to a halt and I was back at my
familiar stomping ground—work. I was savoring the thoughts of
a blessed Mother's Day. Mississippi Mass Choir was assuring and
comforting me that I have power. Yes, Holy Ghost Power. This
past weekend brought with it a second Mother's Day away from
Buffalo, New York. For my family it meant accepting that we
were away from grandmothers for my son, and for my husband
and me, we were not present with our mothers. Gifts were sent
and phone calls exchanged, lengthy conversations were layered
in love and assurances that all was *okay and yes, we love you and
are praying for you.* The phone receivers were hung up and I felt
so much better knowing our gifts and cards had arrived safely to

their designated destinations. Our loved ones knew we had not forgotten them. God was again demonstrating his faithfulness.

As I sat at my desk, I was reflecting on God's fulfillments to me. He knew I wanted to see my mom, but instead He had something else in store for me on Mother's Day. My mom and mother in-law said they loved us and understood we weren't in Buffalo. So that would suffice.

God sent us a present in the form of a God-fearing woman. Our friend and spiritual mentor, Evangelist Wilma Taylor would celebrate Mother's Day with us. She too was away from her son, whom she loves dearly. On Saturday morning, in walked a sharply dressed woman.

She appeared quite distinguished with her smartly coiffure salt and pepper hair, silver blue jacket, and a hint of makeup, which accentuated her outer beauty. She wore a comfortable sandal and skirt speckled with silver blue designs that nicely pulled her look together. I teased her and said, "Where's the little old lady I knew?" My husband chimed in, "See I told you, you look wonderful." She looked better than wonderful; she looked marvelous when she stepped over our threshold. She carried herself as though she knew who she was and to whom she belonged. I knew God had just sent us a blessing in the form of our friend. We all laughed and I quickly said, "You think it's flattery, but I don't want a thing." We smiled, and looked into each other's eyes. I squeezed her and fondly kissed her sweet cheek. Our saintly mother figure had arrived.

In walked Wilma Taylor (yes, one of the contributing authors from *Sister To Sister*, Judson Press) and in walked peace, in walked a blessed assurance, in walked wisdom. In walked a mother, a friend, a loved one who would help me sort out awkward feelings and "make it plain" as the old folks say.

New life sometimes brings new feelings of disenchantment

and uncertainties. This woman of God shared her wisdom and enlightened me on many things; her insight was able to cast new light when I knew there must be more. Our friend, this woman of grace carries the love of God in her bosom. She is an evangelist, loves Jesus and can preach the best preachers under the table. What is such a treat about her is that she's soft-spoken, natural, herself. Her words are not accusative, mystical and angry. Like her summons, her conversations are grounded in God's truth. You couldn't help but appreciate her wisdom and candor. The added bonus is she is full of fun—so with conversing, easy laughter rolls out of her.

During her visit, Wilma assured us that God was directly in our plans when we moved; *Why, He was the center of the plan!* She further pointed out that my husband's ancestors were here where we are presently establishing roots. We are connected and it's no coincidence that we find ourselves in Virginia. And all I needed to do was to take a look at how God had linked and provided countless opportunities for blessings and then said, "God's got so much more in store for you." I knew she was accurate. I could feel it deep down. I can't quite articulate this new feeling of absolute assurance that I feel about the good that God has in store for us. Wilma concurred that what we are now experiencing is the favor of God over and over.

Can you envision that God is at the center of your plans? Can you embrace that faith?

I shared instances when our water was shut off. We were new to Virginia Beach and unaware of Hampton Roads Utility Services a.k.a. HRUBS. In New York State, paying for water was foreign to us, except annually. We awoke to find a tag hanging on our doorknob for the entire world to see for lack of payment. My husband and I frantically rounded up our can of coins and emptied out our then savings account and raced to the utility office to pay the bill. (I didn't want my child to return home from school and there would not be water.)

This by no means would be our last encounter with shut-offs or termination notices. But God has helped us to handle each obligation. Wilma said, "It prepares you for Ministry. Do you know how many times Ministers encounter that?" She then smiled at me. I said, "There were instances when our freezer was down to a package of meat and the can goods were just about gone, and we met a wonderful woman who loved God. She asked, "Do you all need food?" This wonderful woman has a homeless shelter and often needed volunteers to do everything from provide administrative assistance to transportation. Prior to that question, God would send my husband to her aide, he read that her ministry needed assistance and helped her before going to his *paid job*. In turn she blessed us with the needed food and now we help feed others. Our freezer hasn't been empty since. Wilma confidently said, "See how God connects you?" Wilma and I concurred while driving, laughing, eating and leisurely strolling that God opens up floodgates for His provision. He is masterfully orchestrating everything for our good especially during those hard times of poverty, loneliness, debt, loss, hunger, and whatever else life brings.

> "Even youths grow tired and weary and young men stumble and fall, but they that wait upon the Lord will renew their strength…"
>
> Isaiah 40:31

Wilma shared that during a particular offering people sometimes give jewelry and money and place it in the offering plate. These individuals are feeling especially touched by the word of God and desire to express their gratitude. Possibly they have no money,

LINDA MOSE MEADOWS

just the jewelry they are wearing. On one such occasion, Wilma stated that in an envelope was a silver bracelet, it was quite lovely. She didn't think much about it. One day she decided to put it on her wrist, and while eating out, there was a waitress who admired the bracelet from a distance.

Eventually the waitress came to Wilma's table and commented on the exquisiteness of it. This waitress commented that her mother would love this bracelet and asked where Wilma had acquired it. She stated that she said she knew not where it was purchased. Before my friend finished her story, I began to sob, uncontrollably. I knew Wilma had given the waitress her newly acquired bracelet. My friend had given a gift. A wonderful gift that someone knew was of value and was expressing her appreciation for the way Wilma delivered God's word. Wilma had been generous in her sharing—she placed no limitations on giving.

Her example was exemplary of how Jesus does us. He knows no limitations in providing gifts to those of us that believe in Him. I am learning this lesson and consequently am a recipient of good on every turn. When we no longer have a particular need—yes you've got it but, others do, go on and give from your heart and you bless others the way you've been blessed.

> "Give, and it will be given to you! A good measure, pressed down, and shaken together and running over, will be poured into your lap. For with the measure you use, it will be measured to you"
>
> Luke 6:38

Yes, God is faithful in every way.
Good morning!

Listening Intently

"Good and upright is the Lord; therefore he instructs sinners in his ways. He guides the humble in what is right and teaches them his way. All the ways of the Lord are loving and faithful for those who keep the demands of his covenant."

Psalm 25:8–11

I have come to appreciate light bulb moments more. Those are the moments when things come together for you before it begins to make sense. Times when you realize God wanted you to take notice or experience a certain situation. You begin to listen more intently and understand that you must pay better attention next time. God is trying to tell you something. (Remember Miss Ceily in *The Color Purple?*) I would like to believe on my lucid days, days when I am less preoccupied with my concerns and more receptive and open to God's will. He plants thoughts and knows I will ponder them and listen intently for my next direction. But admittedly, there are more days when I am not listening so closely and miss the lesson totally. I am learning to listen more intently to others and myself. I am not so quick to dismiss my feelings or observations. I don't overlook what appears to be obvious to me. I am learning not to always be outspoken, but observant. The obvious will be revealed sooner or later.

Can't you sense when something isn't quite what it appears to be? Often, my friends will come to me in confidence and share a concern. On those days, I would have had a hunch they needed to talk. They, like me, want to appear to have it together, in control. And why not? We are at work? We don't want the world to see us scramble and quake. So we internalize our spoken hurts and harbor them. But, they do seep out in our attitudes, in our conversations, and in our thoughts. But a spoken word, an edifying word can become a healing balm, soothing to the ears and the soul.

Those of us that seek out counsel are looking for support.

We come with our heart in our hands, trusting, believing and hoping that we've gotten life's messages right. We seek each other out for clarification, asking ourselves, *Did I understand that?* Or, *Is that what they meant to say?* We then listen intently for answers.

Often it's not readily apparent. But after we exchange the pleasantries and dance around the files, we get to the heart of the matter. I listen, reflect, tell them what the old Linda would have done, but then, I encourage them not to do that and then express what I believe God wants them to know about the situation. Prayer and encouragement are vital to all of us.

As an adult, it's challenging to be honest, open and listen to things that I just don't want to hear. I listen with my eyes and ears open. We express ourselves in so many ways. Although we have the ability to speak, our words" don't always express our actions. You know the saying, "Actions speak louder than words?" We're human and that's just how we sometimes were created with contradictions. The beauty of it all is that there is always room for growth.

Of course you've figured out by now that sometimes I receive my best inspirations or reflections when I am conversing with my colleague en route to the ladies room. Today I thought about how I see myself relative to aging. It's such a shock to me that I'll soon be forty-five. Isn't that considered midlife? I hear people talk about middle age but I don't quite grasp that that's where I am already. How do you see yourself? In retrospect, I know that I am an adult.

So you wonder how my reflection radiates the thought of listening intently. I asked God that question myself. Here's what God showed me

Every time my husband or son calls my name or speaks in an endearing tone, I listen intently and realize who I am to them— mother, provider, confidante, wife, companion, lover etc. But is that really who I am? When the phone rings and it's my mother and brothers, I am Lynn or sweetie. I am my mother's child, and my brother's sister. I am comfortable with being that. Why it seems, I've been that all my life, a daughter and sister. More recently I am an Aunt, Aunt Linda. That's a blessing. There are days I long for conversations with my nephew and nieces—to listen intently to their squeaky voices. While growing up, it was clearly expressed by my folks that I was a capable, quick learner, trustworthy, responsible, loving, and also loved.

I haven't heard all those affirmations as an adult. Unfortunately, as adults we've had to filter through hidden messages and sort them out. In the world of work and socials, endearing terms are foreign. The labels can range from, driven to incompetent to crazy. (Just know that if the messages were crazy, it was reflective of the world.) We have all experienced unworthy and heart-breaking messages more than we care to even think about. Sometimes the messages were subtle, but more often the negative messages blind-sided us and remained lodged in our psyches. Those self-defeating messages are the ones we mentally replay and intently listened to for breakfast, lunch and dinner. They are designed to defeat us. Those slanted, tainted messages are confusing, and contradictory to what our loved ones said we were. Know that the enemy orchestrated it so those messages were deliberately in earshot, spoken out loud to devalue our human and spiritual worth.

But take heart you who love and believe in Jesus Christ, let me share the message that he brings to all of us who are his beloved children.

> "Behold…my beloved in whom my soul is well pleased"
>
> Matthew 12:18

We are dear to our Heavenly Father. We are worthy servants called, selected, appointed and chosen. Yes that's you and I. God's love is so tremendous, that he sacrificed his only son for us. Out of that deep love, came a sacrificial act of Jesus dying, bleeding, suffering and rising for you and me!

Hear the words of the scripture that says:

> "Greater love hath no man than this that he lay down his life for his friends"
>
> John 15:13

Intently hear this, that you are God's best, when you know that it was He who made your living, breathing and loving possible. He saved your life, your very soul! Our great God, Jehovah desires that you live, speak and hear His truth. Read the Bible for yourself on a daily basis. Read out loud the passages that empower you. Let your ears be filled with deep affirmations—affirmations that speak of His excellent name to all the earth.

"Let them praise the name of the Lord, for his name alone is excellent"

Psalm 148:13

Just as my loved ones instilled my self worth, Jesus desires to instill agape love into the core of your being, your spirit.

Imagine for a moment, His love is a greater love, for your higher calling.

HEARING FROM GOD

"Hear my prayer, O Lord; listen to my cry for mercy.
In the day of my trouble I will call to you, for you will
answer me."

Psalm 86: 6–7

I t was early afternoon; the sun was streaming through the hall
window at work. Standing in front of the centrally located hall
printer, I felt the urgency to pray. A prayer for strength must be
the answer, silently of course. Little did I know God had something else in store! My prayer was chalked full of *thank-you's* (oh!
I was sure I started out correct), then in my spirit, I slowed down,
concentrated and began to earnestly pray. My eyes were wide
open and as I prayed, the copier released my paper. I was standing there waiting.

Apparently, God was getting me ready. I stood there in prayer,
I remembered my child, my teenager saying that he was stressed
yesterday and before he could actually complete his thought—I
chimed in and said, "Yep, I know what that's like." When I stop
to reflect; my son was feeling "bad" because my husband and I
made the decision to not allow him to participate on the tennis team. His Math and Science grades are suffering and tennis
could wait. Our decision to do that is not the point. The point is
I failed to stop and listen when my son wanted to express openly
what was bothering him. Later on I would learn this. During
my prayer I asked God to forgive me for not listening, instead of
interrupting.

My husband came to mind. I also interrupted him during
the time he was instructing and correcting our son. I heard in
the spirit *take your own medicine*. This was not supposed to be

that kind of prayer. Instead, I began to realize that this behavior of interrupting undermines and builds walls of miscommunication between loved ones (the medicine I love to tell others to remember and take). This behavior can do great damage. I now realize that I must take care to demonstrate respect and kindness. Apparently I'm missing the mark in that area. I returned to my desk and humbly asked God to forgive me. *Lord I need help with being over bearing, pushy, judgmental and unkind. Things I never want to think are a part of me. Forgive me if I've hurt my family in any way.* (Maybe I should have asked for forgiveness to include anyone I've slighted or offended.)

We love our families and would like to think nothing they say is trite. I am sure you'd agree that they should be shown honor and respect, even when we don't want to hear the trite. In my "exercise of prayer," God did what he does and that is listen to our petitions. God clearly converses with us. That afternoon, it astounded me. In our Christian journey, we are continually being reshaped to understand the need for "openness" to God's transforming power. God didn't promise change would be easy. During my brief prayer time, I would like to think that in the spirit, God said, *Hold it, and let me share something with you! We will see how "open" you are!*

What resulted was His silently speaking about the areas of my life that needed immediate attention. I was again persuaded to "take your own medicine."

> "Glorious and majestic are his deeds, and his righteousness endures forever. He has caused his wonders to be remembered; the Lord is gracious and compassionate…"
>
> Psalm 111:3–4

LINDA MOSE MEADOWS

So that means as I walk and live in God's holiness, I must also manifest all those things as well—being gracious and compassionate. So as we worship our Lord and Savior, let's remember to 'take your own medicine'. We'll feel so much better and our family will appreciate us for it….we'll experience untold blessings.

Be blessed on this morning. Take care.

A Deliberate Mission

"I remember the days of long ago; I meditate on all
your works and consider what your hands have done"

Psalm 143:5

As I traveled down my neighborhood street and crossed over
the intersection, my teenage son sat silently in the passenger seat appearing to enjoy the ride. No longer were we in Buffalo
and he a toddler, but now we're in Norfolk and there sat a young
man. Our drive brought with it a familiar feeling in an unfamiliar
place. We had had so many trips in the past when it was just the
two of us. He was my traveling companion for a few moments
once again.

I noticed that an elderly gentleman was carefully making his
way; stepping off the sidewalk. He carried a trusted cane and
moved towards us in what appeared to be his reliable vehicle. It
was a seasoned, sturdy vehicle. Much like I imagined he was. My
mother always says, "They don't make cars like that anymore."

The way in which this fine gentleman moved, the old mothers of the church would call it "pressin" or "makin your way."

Yes, this was Sunday afternoon, but the rousing sermons had
concluded and the congregations had long gone home. This man
was taking deliberate steps; he had a mission on his mind. It was
apparent. His coordinated attire and look of determination said
so. He moved with an easy stride, wearing a straw Panama hat;
slightly tilted. He appeared to be tall in stature. His light cream-
colored jacket complemented and matched his trousers and shoes.
Oh, friends he was dressed smartly and determined to reach his
destination. You could surmise he obviously had somewhere to
go; there was a deliberate mission to be accomplished.

Linda Mose Meadows

For a split second, I felt a combination of melancholy and joy at seeing this elderly man. My sweet grandfather, Ellsworth Jackson came to mind. He loved me. We beamed when we were in each other's presence. I can see my Grand Pop so vividly, a Hershey brown man, which huge hands. I would often hold his hands in church. I'd look at him and smile. Years later when he lost his vision, I'd hold his hands and carefully guide him. Touching his hands was deliberate on my part. There was comfort in holding Grand Pop's hand.

We grew so close in my college years at Howard University. Before leaving Buffalo my mama assured me that it was fine to ask my Granny and Grand Pop for whatever I needed. "They are there to help you," she said. My mother left her home in Washington to marry at the age that I was entering college. God knew that two decades later I would have a very special relationship with my beloved grandparents who would provide me with an endless supply of love.

They'd open their hearts, home and wallets whenever they sensed the need. I seldom had to ask. Granny would always press "change" in my hands, and send me back to the dorm with a grocery bag of home baked goodies. When my friends came, she'd do the same for them. Grand Pop would tease me and say, "Little girl, where are you going with all my groceries?" I'd playfully hug and kiss him on the cheek. He'd then say, "Mama gave all my food away again." My mama, his daughter had assured me of this and I was never disappointed. On countless occasions, my Grand Pop would drive up the hill to Howard University in his compact Valiant (with the terrible wheel alignment and no power steering), scoop me and several friends up and off we'd go for the weekend or Spring Recess. They provided us with all the love, nourishment and conversation our hearts could contain. After church, Grand Pop would say, "Go tell your mama (he meant my Granny) that we're going up the country." That meant we were headed up the road from Gaithersburg to Darnestown and Germantown, Maryland. This was an opportunity to see family that I hadn't known or seen since I was a baby. The roads would start out paved and then become bumpy dirt roads. I'd wonder for a moment if we were lost. These hidden places often had no route numbers and formal addresses. If I questioned our whereabouts they might say well we're off such and such road. The defining markers of these homes were post office boxes.

Grand Pop would stop at several cousins' homes. These new faces would greet my Grand Pop with, "Hey Sweetie how's Babe Ruth?" He'd chuckle and introduce me to loving family members and cousins—many were distant relatives and you just knew their family tree had some of the same branches as yours. The voices and other facial features were tell-tale signs. We would enjoy their company and dine sumptuously on their homemade cookies, rolls and jams. Before I knew it, old family photos would appear; the homemade wine would open; and the laughter would begin.

En route to our first destination, Grand Pop would look at me and say, "Honey, you gonna drive?" That was my cue. I'd pipe up, "Yes Grand Pop!" If Grand Pop wanted to have a "taste" of home-made peach or rice wine; he could rest easy—I'd be the designated driver and the thought of chauffeuring my sweet grandfather was too much for my heart to contain. This was the perfect timing I had hoped for. I had just received my driver's license before going off to college and loved driving every opportunity I got.

I might not have ever met Cousin Steve (who was now in his late 90's and blind), Cousin Mead with her sons who all drove corvettes; Punk's and Clegget's people or seen Cousin Jim Branison's land if it had not been for our Sunday sojourns. I saw old home places, family churches, and cousins who had been my grandfather's playmates. They were now seasoned men and women. Grand Pop pointed to new housing developments and empty fields with overgrown bush that were rich in family history. During our travels "up country," I received an education that far exceeded Howard University's classrooms. When I returned to campus refreshed and full, my distinguished professors would know nothing of my continued education.

I treasure my college ring. It represents more than my school; it speaks to me about the love of two wonderful grandparents and a host of family experiences in Maryland and Washington, DC.

I clearly recall it was extremely early in the morning; there was my rotund, sweet, Hershey brown Grand Pop standing. He stood in the dorm foyer, looking as though he was expecting some thing. The person at the desk paged me and said there was a visitor for me. They sounded as though their sleep had been disturbed, I am sure it was dawn. It was, early morning, dark outside. I ran and hugged him—surprised by the sight of my Grand Pop. He had kept his word. He had money neatly folded in his hand. He put it in mine and said, "Honey, here's your money for your school ring." That early morning, like the dapper gentleman I had just seen, Ellsworth Jackson was deliberately going about his business. That morning I was to see my Grand Pop's business. I was a part of that mission. My Grand Pop was coming to see his granddaughter; he beat the early morning Washington, DC rush hour, got to work on time and blessed me with being able to purchase my class ring. His mission was accomplished.

Little did he know that I would carry the gift of his love and our many excursions in the recesses of my joy-filled memories. Thanks to Grand Pop I know about family members that my brothers have only heard of. Grand Pop, Sweetie, Ellsworth Jackson connected me with an invaluable piece of my family heritage. I praise God for this loving man.

Jesus is priceless that way. He will do that for you friend. He will wonderfully connect you with friends, family, and folks you call family—to bless you. You'll look up and discover that you were part of a deliberately designed move of God. Just like my Sunday sojourns with Grand Pop. He introduced me to a part of me I previously knew nothing of.

Jesus has purposeful plans for you as well. He wants to guide and protect you. Strengthen and surround you with a reassurance that your hand is in His hand.

> "For the Lord is a sun and shield; The Lord will give grace and glory; No good thing will He withhold from those who walk uprightly"
>
> Psalm 84:11

Have a good morning.

ALONE TIME

"You are my hiding place; You will protect me from trouble; and surround me with songs of deliverance"

Psalm 32:7

Today I sat at my computer the way I normally do after lunch; except it was not a normal day. Today was a solemn day, a quiet day for many reasons. Our office was not moving in its usual rhythm of hustle and bustle. Staff appeared calm and acted cautious with personal greetings and responses. Many of my colleagues were mourning the loss of a dear coworker. She had died un-expectantly. She had had a seizure while driving, survived; then gone to the hospital was discharged, and later died. I understood she had been challenged with other medical concerns, but her demise was unexpected. You could feel the somberness in the office.

Usually, I am alone in the area in which I work. Actually I was placed in a department that is unrelated to the research and writing that I do. In this department I find myself surrounded by folks; many of who greet me in passing. Some do not even know my name. This department's staff is in the field mainly with issuing licenses, citations and conducting inspections. So you can imagine how it appears as though they are constantly moving and I am alone in my cubicle. Most days that's the case. My work generally has me tied to my desk. It's ok. My past work experiences entailed lots of home visits, running to meetings (using up too much gas), and conducting case conferences, workshops and presentations. I treasure this peace that my being alone provides. Actually, I count it a privilege to be able to stay close to my desk. God has revealed so much to me, in the midst of a routine work assignment that I am sure, I would have missed being in the field. Could it be God's intention, his plan for me—to be alone in this department?

Today was a somber day as well for me. I was beginning my food journal so that I could chronicle and watch my eating patterns; does that ever provide an education. Remember, I plan to combat the early stage of my diabetes. I plan to remain vigilant. I am alone and reflective of what I must do. Instinctively, I reach for the desk drawer of CD's.

My work collection includes: Nancy Wilson, Stevie Wonder, Yolanda Adams, Kirk Whalum and Bee-Bee and Cee-Cee Winans. And let me not forget Donnie McClurkin. Catch me at the right time, you might hear Bach, come back and BB King might serenade you down the hall. Music provides a great escape from my surroundings. It helps to propel me into many assignments that I'm less than enthusiastic about. My hand magnetically became attached to my *Quiet Times Inspirational CD.* God is obviously trying to say something again. This CD was a gift from my wonderful friend, Vivian Reed. She is a Godsend, a woman—generous in her spirit and a joy to be around. She has blessed me on countless occasions—occasions when I felt most alone and vulnerable. She has never reminded me of her giving; never setting me up with the motive of expecting me to reciprocate.

"A friend loves at all times…" (Proverbs 17:17)

I can't share with you what prompted our friendship, our sisterhood. It was an easy connection. It just seems as though she's always been there with an encouraging word or gesture. She's quite about her maturity in Christ and her presence isn't boastful or intrusive. Friends, let me tell you that each time I've needed support or cried unashamedly, she was there. She, her loving husband (Jackie) and daughter actually live around the block from my mother.

When I could not be there (in Buffalo, New York) to make my mother a birthday cake, Vivian was. When I could not be there to hug my mother, Vivian was. When I could not look in my mama's face, my sister and her daughter were able to kick off their shoes and walk around mama's house. Janelle had come to visit her other Granny. It was quite all right to touch and handle whatever she wanted. They believed they were bringing the gifts. Little did they understand that they were the gifts.

Their presence replaced and comforted my concerns about my mother being alone. On another occasion when I had no money to purchase a Christmas gift for my mother and mother-in-law. Yes, Vivian was there ringing the doorbell in thigh-high snow with gift in hand.

"Be imitators of God, therefore, as dearly loved children and live a life of love..."

Ephesians 5:1,2

During my return visit to Buffalo, Vivian shared a CD with me. This was a greater gift than she knew. I remember sitting in her hair salon and hearing her say, "Sister Linda, when I heard this Gospel Jazz CD, it blessed me and I thought of you." She then presented me with this spiritual, soothing music. Excitement is an understatement of what I felt. I was honored that during my alone time in Virginia, many miles away, someone was praying and thinking of my family and me. It had been a year since I had returned to Buffalo. There were more prayers sent up than I realized.

My *Quiet Times Inspirational CD* remains at work. This music has provided me with hours of comfort during long workdays. Often I should have been working but would find myself reminiscing about home and my friends. Did you realize that some music could lift you out of yourself; comfort and inspire you? It has served its purpose well. I urge you to add some anointed music to your collection; it can transform your atmosphere.

In Buffalo, the Meadows and the Reed families would spend many Sundays together. We'd alternate Sundays—taking turns after church and gathering at our respective homes to enjoy each other's company. This family time included barbecues, board games in the yard, sports on the television and beautiful food that B. Smith swore she created. My husband would declare that B. Smith had nothing on his culinary skills. Vivian and my husband would compete with each other in the kitchen. Oh, it was a cook off and it didn't require my lifting a spoon. I loved it. Vivian would get blind-sided by Ricky's delicacies. He might create box brownies and layer it with raspberry jam. It had all the appearances of a gourmet delight. He knew just how to garnish it. His grandmother must have impressed upon him that presentation was everything. Vivian would laugh and respond, "Okay. Meadows, you got me this time, but wait. You tricked me, I didn't smell anything baking." Mission accomplished! Needless to say our families loved eating up the winning meal and looked forward to the next gathering.

Those Sundays in Buffalo are now fond memories. We catch up with each other over the phone and await the arrival of our extended family.

During my adjustment phase, there were many days when I'd experience feelings of being completely alone. Virginia felt foreign to me. It has taken 18 months for me to reconcile that that was Buffalo; this is now Virginia. Thank God, I now confidently call this home with all the loving God planted friendships here in Virginia. I, like you treasure my friends and family. They are gifts from God.

Eighteen months later, I can now appreciate this transition—

this alone time for what God has created it to be. As people of faith, we must not be afraid of being alone; it's purposeful. Know that God always has purpose. If I had only recognized the truth, the truth would have freed me and I would have known—known that my emotions were distorting my view of God's intentions. He was standing right there in the midst of all my fears, all those moments I felt alone. I could not push past my emotions.

> "Which of all these does not know that the hand of the Lord has done this? In his hand is the life of every creature and the breath of all mankind?"
>
> Job 12: 9–10

I am confident in knowing that the enemy wants you to feel abandoned, alone, and defeated. God has said, "Not so!" We are victorious because our Lord and Savior is Jesus Christ.

Your life serves a greater purpose than you know. For many months I was unable to see that although my family arrived here– alone, we were in divine company. Just as Vivian's melodic jazz gospel CD provides comfort. Jesus has provided a comforter just for us. Yes, that's exactly, the Holy Spirit. I encourage you to read your scripture and learn the truth.

Often Vivian will surprise me or I'll get the urge to phone her and we just shout, "You must have heard me thinking about you!" I'll lament that I miss her and she will echo those exact sentiments. I can hear and feel the genuine love that's transmitted over the airways. Our conversation comfortably moves from heartfelt concerns, to a look at what Jesus is doing; before it's over, were crying and praying.

We remind each other through God's words that we are not alone.

"…As I was with Moses, so I will be with you; I will never leave you nor forsake you"

Joshua 1:5

Well friends now that you've read God's word and know the truth, put on your inspirational CD and remember:

"Every good and perfect gift is from above, coming down from the Father…"

James 1:17

One of those gifts is being alone. Have a blessed morning.

THE BLESSEDNESS
OF BELIEVING

"If you remain in me and my words remain in you, ask
whatever you wish, and it will be given you"

John 15:7

I am not actually sure where I want to start with sharing this
good news, but I'll start at home, of course. Several days ago,
my husband said to me, "Girl God's going to give you the desires
of your heart." That statement was said to me while I was brush-
ing my teeth and thinking about what the day would bring. I
didn't expect to hear that, but was appreciative of that declaration.
No sooner had I received it, I began to wonder, *When Lord?*

How often have you heard that statement and wanted to
believe that with all your heart, but your brain does an about face
on you? After my husband announced that, my brain kicked in
the thought, *yes, of course, it's going to happen. I'm just not quite sure
when, but its coming.* So I smiled to myself and moved on to the
next task and filed it for a later time.

As I sit here at my desk, I realize that this has been a phe-
nomenal month for my family. God has done some wonderful
things in the form of unexpected blessings. They were ATP's
(Answers to Prayers). Blessing just seemed to come into our lives
like unexpected guests. They knocked on the door and when we
weren't expecting them, came on in.

These unexpected blessings came in like they were welcomed and oh, indeed they were! Yesterday my husband phoned
me and shared some great news. He told me to lift my hands and
say, "Thank you Jesus"! He then teased me and said, "How can

you lift your hands when you're holding the phone receiver?" I responded, "I'm lifting my hands, one hand at a time, go on tell me." I knew that he's been praying about attending seminary. He saw himself in seminary, saw himself writing and preparing research documents, attending lectures and just enjoying all the things that students love. Yes, my husband has been invited to meet with the president of the seminary. God works just that quickly but often, the waiting for the blessing to materialize becomes the struggle for so many of us. Time and time again, we can witness what God has done for others and ourselves. This is the inspiration for hope.

> "Now faith is the substance of things hoped for, the evidence of things not seen."
>
> Hebrews 11:1

So I am sure you'd agree that there is blessedness of believing. Believing what you can't see. This is faith in action. We will be that much more blessed if we begin to see faith as a foundation for believing in our Heavenly Father.

Well today, the blessedness of believing came to fruition for one of my dear colleagues. She too is a mother like many of us. She has a toddler that she dearly loves and misses during her workday. My son is sixteen years old and her son is two years old. I reminisce, she allows me to do that and then she shares what parenting challenges she's dealing with head on. I listen to her concerns, make several recommendations, she goes home and tries them and on occasion has met good success. We compare other notes and enjoy this sacred time of sharing during work. As I walked by her desk she said, "I guess you've heard." No! Actually I hadn't heard anything, when you don't gossip; people are less inclined to pull you in the circle. Needless to say I observed that the carriers of gossip usually don't want to spread good news, so consequently the news I get is usually old and trickled down. That's fine with me. So I stopped and said, "No!" My friend then announced that in several weeks, she'd be resigning her duties to be at home with her toddler. I was so pleased for her. She was beaming and my eyes were watering; this was a joyful moment.

This had been her hearts desire for quite some time. We had often discussed how important it was to be with our children; mold our children, see then reach critical milestones like reaching for things they had no business, or putting the correct shape into the space, singing silly songs, falling down and getting up without crying and surviving through the potty training days and their determination to sleep everywhere but in their own beds at night. (Oh, there's something joyful about a parent wanting and being able to be with their child and God providing the means to do that.) She was fortunate and blessed to have a husband that could also see the value in this decision.) If you cannot be a stay-at-home parent, that doesn't detract from your worth. Whatever your present circumstances are, God is the authority on good parenting; He'll provide you with the steps that are essential for preparing your children for life.

After my friend shared her news, I looked at her and smiled and said, "Good for you. Your job as mother is the most important work you'll ever have in life." Through this important decision, God was demonstrating to us about the blessedness of believing! There were many days that this young mother wanted to stay home and nurture her child. She longed to take him for walks, now runs (because he's so active), visit the zoo on a less crowded day, watch him run around in his pajamas for an extra hour, bake cookies and play in the yard. My friend's heart sank as she shuffled him off to day care. He stopped crying during the tender drop-off moments at day care and she then became teary eyed instead. She said, "Linda, I know this is the right thing. I have felt such a tugging on my heart." I knew that was the Holy Spirit dealing with her. Not very long ago, she was fortunate to receive the good news that her husband had received a promotion and pay raise. Little did she realize God was obviously preparing her.

My friend was saddened when she expressed that many of her team members had been openly negative. I wasn't surprised. She commented that they wondered how she could afford it. Well, isn't that just like the enemy? Much of what we need for preparing to go out of the home to work isn't needed when you opt to be at home. I assured her that she would do just fine and she had made a wise decision. I did encourage her to be sure to get some time alone to enjoy the things she liked and be sure to talk with other adults. It's vital; mental stimulation is the key.

It's true friends. Do you know the song, "I believe I Can Fly?" Sing it for a moment; out loud is always convincing!

"I believe I can fly. I believe I can touch the sky. Think about every night and day. Turn my midnight into day. I believe I can soar. See me walking through that open door, believe I can…Fly"

Friends embrace the truth about believing. Believe, see yourself doing_____(You fill in the blank), visualize all the steps and activities involved, and I declare that if you believe and hold dearly to that belief, God will bless you so tremendously. You'll begin to think it's always been that way.

Like my husband says, "God's going to give you the desires of your heart, just you wait and see."

"As soon as Jesus heard the word that was spoken, he saith unto the ruler of the synagogue, Be not afraid, only believe"

Mark 5:36

Have a good morning.

Coaching

"All this comes from the Lord Almighty wonderful in counsel and magnificent in wisdom."

Isaiah 28:29

This cool clear Monday morning brought with it an unexpected request—a request I had not anticipated from my supervisor. My supervisor is much like many of us that are perplexed by office decorum. You know the behavior that sometimes causes you to scratch your head and wonder. This young woman is warm, compassionate, driven and idealistic about many things. We enjoy commiserating about desiring to work in a harmonious and peaceful environment…seeking to provide a worthy outcome and a good product.

But, too many days are filled with just the opposite. I do believe that many folks come to work battle-fatigued from life, only to carry out their warfare mentality with colleagues during work hours.

Have you heard the saying that goes something like, "You can pick your friends, but not your co-workers?" Unfortunately, there are some difficult people that we sometimes encounter.

They drag their tote bags and modern leather backpacks heavy from contention and strife. These folks we'd never elect to socialize with, let alone interact with but work demands are different. When you see many of them coming, you see a contentious spirit walking right beside them. Their daily work diets consist of bickering, deceitfulness and confusion. Often, it is disguised in an "Oh by the way did you hear?" conversation or at the meeting woven oh so cleverly in the business agenda. Maybe it's in a biting e-mail with several issues that must be included for an upcoming assignment that masks of a cooperative plan. But it's as big as a pine tree, and deadly as a false accusation.

I am relieved to report that this Monday morning was none of that. This was a cut and dry question posed to me: "Can you please help me?" I was too glad to be able to provide assistance to my boss. My supervisor came to me humbly and earnestly. She had a request that I was happy to oblige. I was honored to coach her from uncomfortable-ness to confidence. Jesus does that well, don't you agree?

She needed my assistance in listening to her speech. Not long ago, another opportunity had come when I had needed her to listen to me, except that was a heart felt concern. It was my turn. We who have great faith are learning to do that. Listen with our hearts and those moments will invariably take us from a place of comfort to a place of risk.

Be assured that God is stretching you and me. He desires that we trust Him and risk coaching someone, risk in possibly encouraging someone to believe in their own God-given abilities; risk in our appearing ignorant and that may be all the answers lie within us. But our Heavenly Father is working with us through the end.

As lovers of Jesus Christ, we should be encouraged that we've been prepared to take the ultimate challenge of opening ourselves up to give the gift of compassion. I asked my supervisor if she had she prayed when she wrote her speech. Had she asked God for guidance? She had prayed but, it was not exactly for guidance. Her focus had been to simply get over the task, to get through the drudgery. I pointed out that she was missing the point of the entire process. I felt that this was an opportunity for my supervisor to shine. Shine in highlighting and demonstrating the services that our organization provides to the public. This is an opportunity to step up and expose our service, even during the most inopportune moments.

Providing a service is what God has placed us here for. He has placed us here to edify, encourage, listen and provide assistance if need be. My boss had been requested by her boss to attend a public meeting and provide an overview of our agency's services. For some reason, this request made her feel inadequate. When I reflect on my supervisor's need, it was more about her needing reassurance and confirmation than my listening and giving pointers on public speaking.

My mom recently did that for me from a distance. She phoned me and then kindly reminded me that what I needed, I already possessed for a healthy life style (I realize that this is not of great significance to many, but it motivated me tremendously, now I walk daily. I trust that this will have a positive impact on my life.) In my possession were my sneakers for walking and a collection of nutritional guides for healthy eating. She encouraged me and loved me. I was well on my way. This gentle reminder helped me to acknowledge that I had done it once before, surely I could do it again. My mother had provided the needed coaching. Her call was a Godsend.

Praise the name of Jesus. Look what He did? He was our best selfless coach.

It was now my opportunity to do just what my mom had done the night before. After my coaching, my supervisor was well ready for the task. She had prepared her speech and the information was accurate. The contents flowed and in my estimation she was ready. Her physical appearance was as professional and tight as the message she was to deliver. Despite this she wasn't convinced. I again, listened attentively, suggested minor changes and found additional information to enhance the subject matter; and then encouraged her to scrap the sheets of paper and instead try utilizing index cards to highlight her points. It made for easy reading and these points would act as memory triggers if she chose not to read her information. I further suggested good eye contact, enunciating words, no acronyms and deep breathing. The breathing would help with relaxing and strengthen the presentation. Jumbled information is never good for a listener. She was sailing, ready. I listened for a final reading, providing reflective listening and believed she was ready. Then I shared with her my experiences about public speaking. It was obvious that God had worked through me. It was time to bid her farewell; she thanked me immensely and exited the building.

Friends, don't you see it? Our lesson that God has once again provided to us is that we must step out of ourselves and not hold back in our giving. Jesus provided us with numerous opportunities where He acted as the lowly servant and gave to his disciples. Remember His washing their feet? Jesus excmplified humility at its finest. His highest example is his crucifixion, of course. As He hung on the cross, He still encouraged and coached the thief. Coaching provides us with an opportunity to not only give, but to be obedient and see God's work in action.

Think about it; I could have told my supervisor during the first hour that her speech was fine: "Be on your merry way!" But I would not have been providing her with Godly encouragement and coaching. Isn't that what all of us desire and need during those critical times? Let God use you as He does all of us. Give during the most inopportune times. Give when you least expect it, and go the extra mile. God will continue to bless you for your obedience.

By the way after my supervisor gave her presentation, she phoned me and thanked me profusely; she recounted that many of the official meeting attendees acknowledged her good work. My supervisor approached me and said, "Please read this." I read a response from a committee member that saluted my supervisor for her work and her graciousness in receiving funds to carry out the mission of our organization. This writer said my supervisor's boss should be proud of such a great representative. I know without a doubt that God was in the plan, as soon as my supervisor said, "Can you help me?" God said, *surely, let me send one of my own to help! Linda, you go and be a blessing, coach her today.* I reminded my boss that God is so good!

> "See I lay a stone in Zion, a tested stone, a precious corner stone for a sure foundation; the one who trust and will never be dismayed"

Isaiah 28:16

Have a good day.

EXPECT
THE UNEXPECTED

"They asked each other, 'Were not our hearts burning within us while he talked with us on the road and opened the scriptures to us?'"

Luke 24:32

Friends, I did not want to expect the unexpected. I did not feel that I needed that lesson, not again in life. My hidden fear is being in poverty, moving to a broken down dwelling, with dashed dreams and miserable, hurting people. I don't want to be victimized; I would like to think that God would not wish any ill experiences upon me. Wasn't moving to Virginia enough—bank accounts depleted, agonizing about rent, turned off utilities and nights of restless sleep?

But the entire picture is anything but that. God works it out on every turn for us. We have never lived, and eaten so well, never had as many positive life changes as we now have in Virginia, with Jesus at the helm. Never have we had to depend on God, like we do now. I would not have it any other way. He has been so gracious, so kind, so open and so on time.

"With a mighty hand and outstretched arm; His love endures forever"

Psalm 136:12

I have not yet experienced eviction, hunger, and destitution. And if I should, that doesn't make me any less of a child of the Great Jehovah. There are surely unexpected trials that will come. Jesus has sustained us and He will. His mighty arm has not forsaken us. We are blessed on every turn and will continue to be if we simply believe in Him and raise our expectations about how God will work in our lives.

I wish I could take credit for that thought. Bishop Milton A Williams shares that encouraging word in his commentary, *Expect the Unexpected* (African-American Devotional Bible NIV).

Didn't it just bless you! Yes, the disappointments will come. Just like each new day, but Jesus is right there walking along side of us, waiting for us to turn our gaze in his direction. Won't you join me as I go though this time of uncertainty about my next paycheck? It will surely come, but in the mean time I will raise my expectations.

> "I will lift up mine eyes unto the hills, where does my help come from? My help comes from the LORD, the Maker of heaven and earth"
>
> Psalm 121:1, 2

Thank you, Bishop and thank you, Jesus!

TIME WELL SPENT

"There is a time for everything, and a season for every activity under heaven…"

Ecc 3:1

It was ironic that on my last day of work for the health department, I would walk to my desk and there to my surprise to see a gift bag in the shape of a rose. Well today, on my birthday, the 45th, I would find a rose there. Inside the bag was a beautiful package of gift cards that had a picture of a cup of tea and scripted on these note cards was the message: *Praying for you as I often do–with a heart full of thankfulness.* Not only were there gift cards in my gift bag, but also there was a lovely book titled, *Living Simply in God's Abundance, Strength and Comfort For the Seasons of A Woman's Life,* by Suzanne Dale Ezell.

Well, friends, you know by now that's who I'm striving to become, a woman who enjoys the simple abundance of living and is unencumbered by seasons of change. I have a great deal of growing in that area. I can say that I enjoy the abundance of laughter with loved ones, admiring nature's bounty (our God can only create this kind of beauty), marveling at the sky and appreciating what it means to be loved. Loved for all my character traits—the good and bad. Life can be chaotic even in the midst of excitement and joy.

"He is like a tree planted by the streams of water which yields its fruit in season and whose leaf does not wither. Whatever he does prospers."

Psalm 1:3

So here I am, crossing over into a brand new dimension, about to encounter another threshold, one I've never experienced, but am full of trust and not nearly as anxious as a year ago about where God will take me.

I am sure He has not brought me this far to drop me like a football into an abyss of pain and uncertainty. Be sure that the enemy wants me to believe this and think it, live in it, and die from it! It is the furthest thing from the truth.

I stumbled upon a treasure in my gift today. Yes, you guessed another inspirational devotional. But I choose to see this title in another light. Let me explain. In this book were the words: *It's Just A Waste of Time.* Those words introducing the devotional struck me like lightening. It hit a nerve, my spirit stood up; I knew God wanted me to know my time at the health department had not just been a senseless, useless exercise. No, it had not been a waste of time.

Admittedly, in my mind the thought came sneaking up, and I would close the trap door to this thought, *Linda you were just spinning your wheels there.* I'd snap that thought shut, slam! Then later the thought would creep back, *you should have taken that job in Chesapeake, even though the pay was less, the security was so much better!* Oh, friends, but I did entertain the thought and gave it more time than it was worth. So you see the title of this devotional had echoed a thought I had had previously on several occasions.

Today in my spirit, I refused to let those negative thoughts diminish my appreciation of Janet's gift and the many other wonderful gifts and out-pouring of love with which my sister friends had surprised me today. I appreciated their thoughtfulness, the gifts meant so much, the words she and others expressed, confirmed what God wanted me know.

He intended for me to experience just a season at the health department. Janice stated that I had encouraged her, and had told me in the past that I had listened to her and assured her on so many turns. I am not sharing this with you for accolades, but as a reminder that God plants us where we are, right where we are for many reasons. Most of the time I have not really had a real understanding on why He elects to place me in jobs that are in the 'helping professions'. My degree is public administration. I long to do just what I am doing now; write, bake chocolate chip cookies, travel and see my family and volunteer when and where I want. Maybe later, He will grant me those things. Obviously, God has me working on some other kind of public administering.

Can you see God's hand in your life's work? Give it some thought and then pray and ask Him for direction. I can begin to see more clearly that we have seasons, spiritual seasons that prompt us, pull us, mold us, break us, and reinforce in us what God intends for us to be. God doesn't ask our consent on when and where our seasons will begin and end. My mother likes to say:

> "Well Lynn, we are in the process of becoming. There is a time for everything, and a season for every activity under heaven: A time to be born, and a time to die; a time to plant, and a time to uproot, A time to kill, and a time to heal; a time to tear down and a time to build, A time to weep, and a time to laugh; a time to mourn, and a time to dance; A time to scatter stones and a time to gather them a time to embrace, and a time to refrain, A time to search and a time to give up, a time to keep and a time to throw away, A time to tear and a time to mend ; a time to be silent and a time to speak; A time to love, and a time to hate; a time of war, and a time of peace. What does the worker gain from his toil? I have seen the burden God laid on men. He has

made every thing beautiful in its time. He has also set eternity in the hearts of men; yet they cannot fathom what God has done from beginning to end. I know that there is nothing better for men than to be happy and do good while they live. That everyone may eat and drink and find satisfaction in all his toil-this is the gift of God. I know that everything God does will endure forever; nothing can be added to it and nothing taken from it. And also that every man should eat and drink, and enjoy the good of all his labor, it [is] the gift of God. God does it so that men will revere him" (Ecclesiastes 3: 1–15)

Isn't God's word clear? While at the health department, I would grow, and take on some difficult tasks many I'd never before encountered, some I'd excel in and others I might miss the mark and fail. But, it did not kill me while on this journey, in this season.

I now reflect and see that during that season I was growing in grace, learning more about the health profession, encouraging others and being encouraged along the way.

So I have to thank God, that I've grown up enough in these last eighteen months in Virginia, not to crumble when one season ends and another begins. I give thanks that I now know that this is apart of the life we live as believers in the gospel, no matter what the circumstance dictates. God said *no good thing will He withhold from me.* That *me* is inclusive of you. You'll find that in the scripture.

I have to believe that because I am bought with a price. You know Jesus gave up Himself, for our eternal life. As believers we are required, it's mandated that we trust the very God who controls the universe. We are His and must live according to His laws.

It is then safe to adopt the attitude, *Life come on with your best shot! Because my Jesus has assured me that I will live triumphantly.* So if this is indeed the case, you and I can embrace the changing seasons of winter, spring, and fall. Only God could do that!

God is our change agent, and He rules the universe. Remember singing the song, This is Father's World? Go on and hum it as you start your great day.

May God bless and keep you.

THE ONLY THING
THAT COUNTS

"…The only thing that counts is faith expressing itself through love".

Galatians 5:6

I wanted to do nothing but concentrate on what I had just read. This spiritual commentary was not over my head, you understand not particularly heavy, but it bore a particular weight that I just didn't want to examine at 10:30 a.m. The subject matter of emotional burdens was not my forte this morning. *Please God why?* I am sure my psyche was defiantly proclaiming that statement.

This morning was a slow morning, no job to run off to, or deadlines to meet. It had been so long since I had this kind of leisure time that it was unfamiliar and discomforting to me. I didn't want this leisure time, not on these terms. My mind was racing; I needed to be occupied. I could clean up my bedroom, there were books, papers, magazines in every corner; clean clothes that sat in a piled high laundry basket, pairs of shoes everywhere but where they should be and linen to be changed. Nope! I didn't have to tackle that; my husband had assured me that he would help me, which meant I could ignore the bedroom till later.

Okay so now what Lord? I am sure, He said, *Linda, go and read. You need to focus on a good word today. A word from me.* So I thought, *Okay, in a few moments God.*

I groomed, applied my makeup, got dressed and listened as my morning radio show concluded. Surprisingly, the next song playing was Yolanda Adams's singing:

"This battle is not yours, it's the Lord's. No matter what you're going through. Remember God is only using you. This battle is not yours. It's the Lord's. It's the Lord's. Hold your head up high…"

Coincidence, well you know better. God showed me, I could take my time if I wanted; He'd assured me of His love anyhow. God was informing me through Yolanda's song to have faith, and let Him handle this spiritual battle. Still not feeling totally convinced, nor persuaded yet, I focused on my next steps—of getting breakfast, doing some laundry and answering the phone, in that order and oh yes, squeezing in an inspirational reading.

Can't you see the procrastination? My spirit was not completely cooperating. But, deep down, I knew that message was just for me. Yolanda's song on the radio was the furthest thing from a coincidence. My stomach's nagging, gnawing sensation wouldn't let up. This hidden emotion was all too familiar. It's an old friend that I knew as a little girl when my parents argued; in college when my courses were a struggle; during my divorce when I wondered what would become of me and my infant son; during recent years of balancing rent with utility payments; when a bill collector phoned; when a grant or work assignment must be completed and the deadline is near; when I need to express myself and won't; when enough is too much. Yes, this emotional discomfort and disappointment translates itself into a stomachache that latches on and won't let go. I seldom admit that this is occurring.

But much to my surprise today, things would be different. I would embrace the truth and know that although I just couldn't shake this feeling:

"…The only thing that counts is faith expressing itself through love"

Galatians 5:6

You wonder what that means. Let me show you how God revealed this to me and notice if that doesn't explain what this scripture implies. There, it sat on my kitchen table a copy of my *In Touch Magazine* from July 2002…having recently received in the mail. I had overlooked it, but this was obviously the right time. So, as I ate my bran flakes with sliced strawberries, swallowed my hypertension tablet, drank my juice, I began to read Charles Stanley's commentary entitled, "The Burden of Emotional Baggage." It was such an appropriate reading; I got up to check the dryer for laundry, folded clothes and threw in another load. Charles Stanley struck a profound cord that I wasn't ready to tackle.

God was at it again, I knew full well what He was doing to me. He made me pay attention and get to the root of my discomfort. Yes, right there at my own kitchen table.

It was much like the experience I had just had upstairs in my bathroom while grooming and looking at my own reflection in the mirror. There I stood, applying makeup, grooming and dressing not dealing with the source of my gnawing, aching stomach. I didn't even stop to pray. Yes, masking and ignoring the obvious.

I was emotionally caught up in my anguish. Hurt that things weren't just a tad bit different. Hurt that I was unemployed and feeling all the uncertainty that accompanies being out of work. An old familiar emotion came to take safe harbor; and God was not going to stand for it not another day. So, I could do everything to be busy, by eating cereal, dressing slowly, and even folding and washing clothes. God redirected my steps and made me address my emotional baggage issues this Monday morning, with my sanctified, give you a good word self!

I would have to empty all my luggage of hidden emotions right before your eyes today. There's no need in me asking myself, *did I have to?* Because, *Yes, I did!*

God is urging me to persuade you to do the same. Recognize that our emotions can spur us on to great heights or cripple us, hinder us and cause us years of heartbreaking confusion. We do have choices just as Charles Stanley has pointed out to either let the emotions control us, or be controlled by us. If we embrace the former philosophy we'll miss out on God's faith moves. We'll be so consumed by the bitter experiences, that we won't live a life led by the spirit.

> "But the fruit of the spirit is love, peace, patience, kindness, goodness, faithfulness, gentleness and self-control."
>
> Galatians 5:22,23

So come on friends and join me, leave your emotional baggage on the curb and embrace a new, a powerful freedom in Christ Jesus and live by His Holy Spirit. The Holy Spirit pointed out that just a moment ago; I couldn't deal with the truth about the gnawing pain in my stomach.

Emotional baggage serves a purpose that's not of God. The express design of the hidden baggage or hurts we carry is to overtake us, do us in and kill any attempts to build our faith. As the kids say, "It's blocking!"

Remember we grow from one level of faith to the next. So the familiar emotion that says you and I won't succeed comes in the form of a dull stomachache, pain or negative behavior. For me, I've had that dull stomach ache since I was a child overhearing my parents. Admittedly those were some upsetting moments; listening to grown-ups argue, experiencing my own divorce, completing college requirements, living with financial strain, and you fill in the blanks.

But the truth is like you I, survived all of it, and most of those times were met with blessed outcomes and sweet success. I can say to you that the love of God kept me and brought me to this point that I now write and share with you!

Apostle Paul writes in Galatians 5 that we should mark his words, and not abandon the principle of God's grace that brings salvation—salvation that is a living faith in a loving God. And we know that our faith is expressing itself through the love of our savior. Imagine that, don't you feel better already!

Take heart and let us embrace the truth free of the heavy emotional baggage that:

> "The only thing that counts is faith expressing itself through love…"
>
> Galatians 5:6

Have a wonderful day.

GOD'S COMPLETE LOVE

"But if anyone obeys his word, God's love is truly
made complete in him. This is how we know we are
in him: Whoever claims to live in him must walk as
Jesus did"

I John 2: 5, 6

After reading my scripture of I John regarding God's Love
and Ours. I topped it off with another favorite devotional,
which focused on maintaining joy in Jesus; wouldn't you know it,
out fell my Virginia Natural Gas bill. My memory kicked in and,
I recalled that I needed to make another installment payment on
an overdue gas bill. There were several bills inside the envelope.
One bill stated in bold letters **Deposit Installation Turn Office
Notice and the other bill simply stated in bold letters. Turn Off
Notice**. When the bills were sent to us, I was appalled that the
Installation bill was created not because we had not paid, but
because Virginia Natural Gas didn't appreciate our slow method
of payment. What could we do other than what we'd been doing,
paying when we could? This was not our sandbox and these were
not our toys. Unfortunately consumers don't make the rules, they
just accept the rules—or go without.

I phoned my husband as I normally do, when I am stressed.
I've stopped holding all that in, now I share all of my concerns.
Lord I want a new subject! Yes, that's what I said to my husband
as I hung up the phone. It was not an angry tone, just the realization that I needed to mentally move on. I am tired of feeling as
though the bills have me in a headlock. I envision them wearing wrestling caps and leotards and I am losing in the wrestling
match.

Why can't I seem to grasp this demon and win? I excel at reassuring others; can't you hear me telling them that these things are minor afflictions? Why can't my psyche accept this pep talk and get with the program? I was at work, and needed to do that, not negotiate with the utility company another payment plan, run out at lunch time, zoom to Farm Fresh (for your convenience you can grocery shop and pay your utility bills), make the payment, and run back through the doors, call the utility company representative and have indigestion throughout the afternoon. Or I could simply ignore them and suffer through the cold-water showers. No, No I don't want to endure either predicament.

Just this morning, my husband and I had had a brief discussion about the utility bills. My husband hadn't seen the bills for the month. I stated in a not so sweet response that I had not hidden them; they were in the bill basket. The bill basket is located on the backer's rack with my favorite cookbooks. It's that an oxymoron. No wonder I don't enjoy looking for new recipes, the bills are obstructing my view.

I have a collection of baskets. You name it—it's stored in baskets. Vitamins and cough remedies, bread and baked goods, cosmetics, batteries, remote controls, magazines, important papers and kitchen drawer clutter. I have baskets full of goodies. They are attractive and store things well. So they serve a good purpose. That's my rationale anyway. So, yes you guessed it. There's also a basket full of bills.

Bills honestly are overwhelming to me. I hate them and I hate focusing on them. Our budget is limited. We are able to pay tithes, rent and purchase the essentials. Consequently our payment method has become whatever gets our attention first that's what we focus on. We've done ok thus far and I know God's grace allows us to receive extensions and payment plans. I deliberately try not give the bills too much of my attention, because I don't want to be pulled in an undertow of depression because of bills. I have done all I know to do. But that dreaded wrestling match occurs—paying a few bills and overlooking many.

I hope you realize that often it's not until I am writing you, that I get it. Then I understand what God is relaying to me. Well once again that has happened. It was no mistake that I read what I did this morning God's Joy. We should have joy because of His Salvation. God knew the events that would follow my devotional reading. In a few moments my focus had gone from joy to gloom.

> "Yet I will rejoice in the Lord, I will be joyful in God my Savior"
>
> Habakkuk 3:18

Why didn't I do that instinctually? Too many baskets I guess. God initially reminded me in my devotional reading time, which yes, *Linda there are more bills than you and Richard can currently handle, but there's joy in me, I am your salvation.* God then backed that statement up with:

> "We know that we live in him and he in us, because he has given us of his Spirit. And we have seen and testify that the Father has sent his Son to be the Savior of the world. If anyone acknowledges that Jesus is the Son of God, God lives in him and he is God. And so we know and rely on the love God has for us"
>
> I John 4: 13–16

If we are not careful the bills can become bigger that our love of God; bigger than our joy of Salvation; bigger that our love for one another; bigger than our faith walk with Jesus. Your baskets possibly, may be filled with something else that is detrimental to your spiritual and physical life. Take an honest assessment and begin to pray and ask God for assistance in that area. What we must be careful to do is not let the enemy steal and manipulate our focus, which results in our doubting that:

> "…God lives in us, and his love is made complete in us"
>
> I John 4: 12

Please go back a few verses and get this deep in your spirit:

> "You dear children are from God and have overcome them, because the one who is in you is greater than the one who is in the world."
>
> I John 4:4

Even when our baskets of discomforts are overflowing we are so complete in God's love. Remember we are overcomes of the world because of our faith in Jesus Christ our Lord. I'll see you at Farm Fresh.

Have a joyful day friends.

A HEALING BALM

"Is there no balm in Gilead? Is there no physician there? Why then is there no healing, for the wound of my people?"

Jeremiah 8:22

So much had happened this past weekend it's difficult to chronicle. Yes there was the cookout, more than enough potato salad, all the traditional fixings, and the fire works, friends from home and some surprise emotional ups and downs that were so upsetting that they could not be ignored.

The emotional roller coaster had taken both my husband and I for quite a journey. It really started with me on Saturday. I sat on my deck admiring the wonderful breeze and easiness of the day. I decided I needed to relax and that's what I did. As I read a novel that I had recently purchased at a festival in Hampton. I examined the cover, read the story line, and admired how this young author sat alone at her table, without any umbrella, tent or any visible sign of support. This was just last weekend. I could see her face, she appeared to be cheerfully autographing her novel, and chatting with anyone that was interested. Her visibly slumped posture was contradictory to her greeting. (I didn't want to focus on that.) I admired her devotion to her creation, but wondered what she must be thinking. I asked her how sales were going. She replied, "Great!" I then said, "Good for you and I'd like to buy your book, also."

So there I now was reclined on my chaise, reading her book and reflecting on my new station in life, my distant friends, my loved ones and how another holiday weekend I would find myself somewhere I totally had not expected.

As I read the story I would learn that the main character of the story had been in an abusive relationship, which would eventually fizzle, not soon enough. From this relationship she'd received verbal messages of defeat and hate.

Unfortunately, she internalized so much of it and carried those hidden messages in her heart. She would then become involved with a man who was her soul mate, but discover that she had breast cancer. In sorting all of her hurt regarding the cancer, she'd reject this man that truly loved her.

The rejection was out of fear and her anger about the disease and her internalized messages that she was unworthy of love. As I read, tears began too flow, yes the story was sad, and there were things about this character that could ring true for all who are suddenly faced with a life threatening disease. But that's not really what I was crying about. I cried because I too felt sad, I cried because although my wonderful husband was just a few steps away—I missed my loved ones, my friends who knew all about me and could encourage me or tell me to get with the program. I cried as I sat in an absolutely peaceful place but needed something that only God could provide. Yes, a healing balm to soothe all my hurts. My husband came out onto the deck and said, "Honey what's the matter?" I could only shake my head, I said, "I don't know." Then I thought and said, "This is a beautiful place, but it sure is lonely."

The very next day my husband and I were met with some unkind looks and uncooperative behavior regarding work in the ministry. Oh, but it did and it continues to happen. It's contradictory to Christian Ministry. Imagine! So my husband and I have continued to pray that we not behave Un-Christ like. We sort through the confusion, and vowed to give no more conversation to this negative behavior. We touched and agreed, held on to each other, said we'd throw away the hurt feeling, dash the negative mental tape recorders, smiled at each other and vowed that enough was enough.

Friends, you do know just because you say you're through with something doesn't mean God is! So our wonderful friends invited us over for dinner, we declined because our other friends extended a dinner invitation, but my husband chimed in, "We'll come later for desert." We arrived much later than we expected and was greeted by our Mother Queen at the door. Our friends were resting, some family members had gone out and the guests were a fond memory. My husband and I agreed we should visit another time. Mother Queen opened her door and her arms. She immediately hugged us and said, "No come in, I am glad you came. I asked where you were for dinner." We both smiled, we knew we were welcomed.

I could instantly feel the peace as I stepped over her threshold. The house was lingering with good smells of a dinner that I am sure was greatly approved and appreciated. We sat at her kitchen table, enjoyed ice cream, cake and happily conversed. We laughed about many things, explored growing up and what family love really meant.

God was up to something and I believed we were just visiting on a Sunday evening. Mother Queen was a part of this master plan and just possibly she might have detected the weariness that we carried.

I would like to believe the hurt we buried was not so transparent, but God knew what was in our spirits. When I reflect on how sweetly she embraced us, I know that we where a part of a divine appointment. Can't you just see it? It was nothing but the love of God that brought us to her door, sat us at her table and then allowed us precious uninterrupted time with her.

Mother Queen's outpouring of love-helped transform our

hurts into healing. She was administering a healing, sanctified love with down to earth soft speech and a holy human touch.

Before leaving my husband opened up and candidly asked Mother Queen her impressions on something that was burning in his heart. Bewilderment, a hurt and he wasn't sure of its motive nor origin. As Mother Queen looked at him and then me, it was as though she was pulling us into her arms with her love. It's the way all mothers and grandmothers do to soothe a scraped knee, a broken heart or a bruised ego. She sat at her table and delicately poured on us her healing balm, her sage wisdom, her reassuring love, her humor and then said, "Don't worry about that that doesn't matter!"

Her Godly wisdom and perspective help make sense of some hurtful, unkind behavior; behavior that had been so puzzling and wrong. When my husband and I left her home, we rode back on a cloud, and thanked God that he'd set this visit up just like it occurred. Friends we were soothed and went home, said a prayer and slept like two content babies that had been bathed and powdered. We awoke still thankful and refreshed.

For those of you who also need a soothing touch, a healing balm and outpouring, down to earth display of love, I pray that you too will find your way to the table of a loving person, sit and eat some ice cream, asking them a burning question you've been carrying in your heart and then watch Jesus show up and show off His healing balm of love. Love, true love is only a touch away.

> "The LORD your God is with you, he is mighty to save. He will take great delight in you, he will quiet you with his love, he will rejoice over you with singing."
>
> Zephaniah 3:17

In Your Name

"Salvation is found in no one else, for there is no other name under heaven given to men by which we must be saved"

Acts 4:12

Why is it that we elect to do certain things in a particular manner? Some might argue, "That's the way we've always done things." Another might say, "It's protocol." I heard an evangelist say, "It's knowing who to call!" That's truly the key isn't it? Having the right connection, the right source, the person with the juice to help you side step the preliminaries and jump right to the source. We want what we want when we want it! And if it's a need we get quite aggressive. We'll generally let nothing get in our way when we have need of (you fill in the blank.)

Life would be so much easier if we could only have the right source. Let me share with you what I learned today, early Monday morning waiting for my reliable mechanic in his backyard. I took my usual seat outdoors under the trees. That's where customers sit in the summer friends. It makes waiting for your car less painful, of course unless it's ninety-nine degrees.

I had a great time conversing with the mechanic that tinkered under the hood of another car; he'd stick his head around the hood and occasionally making light conversation. As my great uncles would say, "He handling his business."

Another friendly, gentleman walked up who was obviously well acquainted with the shop, sat down and began to converse with me and the mechanic under the hood. Oh friends I had a great time laughing with these men. I thought I was in the barbershop for a moment. Mind you there were no vulgarities, innuendos, or uncomfortable conversation. It flowed naturally, and the laughter was good medicine. I was there in the name of getting preventive work on my automobile; the mechanic under the hood was of course there in the name of his profession. And I suspect their friend that was there was stopped in because he had a need to see his friends.

When I reflect on this, I believe we were all there because of a divine appointment.

The friendly gentlemen sitting next to me under the trees said to the mechanic that he attended church on Sunday. He commented that he truly enjoyed service and had initially felt the need to begin again attending regularly. He then said that the church he attended did something that made him feel truly uncomfortable as a guest. The usher marched him up front to the first pew. I purposely used the term march because I could envision this. You're a guest, feeling a little out of sorts, on the spot really, especially if you're alone and then you're taken in front of everyone, surely feeling awkward and now the congregation is staring a whole in the back of your head.

Well this good natured gentleman, now laughed at the thought of this and said, he tried to clap at the appropriate time, when the reader directed the church to follow the text, there was no hymnal and when he was asked to stand a share something about himself, well that was the icing on the cake. After church, one of the members asked him if he was a preacher. The mechanic came from underneath the car staggering with laughter and I couldn't help it. What had occurred to this visiting guest was in the name of what? The mechanic said an identical incident happened to him at another church, said he greeted the guests, but said to them that there hospitality was a little overwhelming, and made him have second thoughts about revisiting. Our conversations then went from gardening, male teen pregnancy to my giving instructions about a lip smacking good Eggplant Parmesan.

I wanted to revisit that church conversation; I couldn't quite let it go. It was my opportunity to applaud this man's conviction to reconnect with a church home and commended his courage in attending any church of his choice. I then shared with him about the death of my dear friend's husband and the loved he showed for his wife. His concern before he transitioned from earth into the everlasting arms of Jesus was to make certain he had established a relationship with Jesus and brought others to the knowledge of Christ. His final days of living were to encourage others to receive Salvation in the name of Jesus. After sharing that with this divine acquaintance, I encouraged this kind man to continue to attend church, put his hand up, for the halt sign to the usher and say to him or her where his seating preference was, but more importantly to develop a closer walk with Jesus because that's what all of our business was about today, was to reflect why we do what we do in the name of worship service, love, hospitality and (you fill in the blank).

Have a blessed day friends.

JESUS SAVES

"And to know that this love that surpasses knowledge that you may be filled to the measure of fullness of God. Now to Him who is able to do immeasurably more than all we ask or imagine, according to His power that is at work within us; to Him be glory in the church and in Christ Jesus throughout all generations, for ever and ever! Amen."

Ephesians 3:19–21

God "messed me all up today!" or in our everyday language "Was I ever surprised today!"

You realize that I now have young people around me (College age and High School) so I am learning more of their expressive language and imagine I get it! Ok, maybe just a little of it! But, admittedly, I am very green. Yes, impressionable too.

"Messed up," connotes surprise, something totally unanticipated, an unexpected or strange occurrence. I am sure a young person might describe the nature of events this morning in those terms.

After enjoying our Sunday brunch-styled breakfast prepared today, Friday, with my stepson and our newest adopted child who's attending college, it was my intention to juggle washing a load or two of dirty clothes, sit at the computer and type several hand written devotionals that were long overdue for print. It was going to be a "work at your own pace kind of morning."

But my flow was momentarily disrupted. No it was abruptly disrupted! The contractors returned this morning and were walking around in my space like they were home, hammering, dragging dusty tarps up and down the stairs, lifting windows and letting in the all out doors. Insects had made themselves a new home! And the workmen were just being a plain nuisance in my space, my comfortable domain. It seemed every time I looked up there was another unfamiliar body carrying a tool or a paintbrush.

"Not again Lord, who might this be?"

The caller identification box that strategically is placed among my teapots and saucer collection stated anonymous call. I truly did not want to pick up the telephone receiver, but I must have had a teenage moment, you know how the phone rings once and you wonder *what is their rush? Why can't they let it ring or for that matter let the answering machine get it!?* I must have forgotten all of that! I snatched the phone up and much to my surprise it was my sister-in-law.

She was phoning from Buffalo and I was delighted to hear her voice. We chatted and laughed about how God had intervened and done it again. Her nephew, my stepson had been blessed by unexpected source his grandfather.

Glory to God, what a wonderful interruption!

My stepson would be receiving the required initial payment to give him a jump start to start the semester at Tidewater Community College. It was as plain as the strangers walking around my home with tools—that God had moved mountains, hearts and opened minds in behalf of this young man.

Jesus had saved the day again!

One day Courtney needed the tuition and the next it had already been worked out. Here's another time that JESUS stepped in and Saved! Prayers were answered instantly. I don't know that my stepson can comprehend it right now. But God's saving grace is so timely.

So you wonder what I was referring to about being "messed up?" Let me explain how God had me to know that again, He Saves!

He saves during our most vulnerable moments when we don't have a clue on what to do. We look to the left or the right and it appears that God is so far out of our reach. From all accounts it appears that God does not want to know us, hear from us or see our need.

Our Heavenly Father loves us and will surely step in. Jesus can save us from our pitiful circumstances and ourselves.

Believers we must hold on to the hope that God is there and about to visibly break forth, burst on the scene with a plan you could not fathom or orchestrate.

During my phone conversation, I was listening to my spiritual CD's when the phone rang. In the background was the *Daryl Coley Live in Oakland: Home Again with the New Generation Singers Reunion Choir.* The moment the phone rang the song Jesus Saves began playing. The more our conversation moved in the direction of how awesome God is and moves, the more my throat began to close and tears came to my eyes.

Jesus continues to save me and answer my prayers over and over again.

I am sure you too know that God freely gives to believers. We have the benefits of His divine glory! You know my stepson has a group of faith filled men and women of God praying on his behalf.

Friends, God does nothing in secret, nor does He hide his hand. He'll display your blessings for the world to see. I have heard it said that His signature is all over our lives.

Thank you Lord. My soul cries Holy, Halleluiah!

During today's phone conversation, it was as though there was a group of spiritual cheerleaders singing and echoing these exact sentiments that Jesus Saves!

Daryl Coley sings it best in the song so aptly titled Jesus

Saves. I got so caught up in the music that I began to only type snippets of the song:

> "Jesus saves! Hey, Oh yes, He does! I am so glad, He says who so ever will come. To the utmost, oh yes He does! To the inth degree that means He saves everybody! Jesus Saves. Let everything have joy! It doesn't matter how low you think you've gone. To the utmost. Nobody can do it like He can. It doesn't matter how far think you've gone away, Oh yes He's all by himself. He can deliver you Aw yes, oh yes He does! Give the words a mighty voice I was sinking in sin, far from the peaceful shore. Very deeply stained within, sinking to rise no more But the master of the sea heard my despairing cry. Can I have joy? Does he love me? Oh Yes! Does he care for me? Oh Yes! Jesus Saves! Let me hear you say it! Oh, yes he does! Jesus saves!"

As my conversation was concluding with my dear sister in law, she mentioned a mutual friend, and I learned that he had recently gotten married. This was again another testament of how our Lord and Savior saves.

You say big deal there are marriages everyday. But had you only witnessed our friend not many yesterdays ago. There he was an admitted mess, walking up and down Bailey Avenue homeless, children removed from him by social services, drug addicted, and lost to the world. But our friend's story doesn't end there—Jesus stepped in!

Our friend's life has evolved and he is a brand new creature, a righteous saved man of God, filled with hope, love and promise. He's a living, anointed epistle, happily married, serving in his community, loving his family and praising God!

Yes, friends we know it, that this morning God wants to convey to us that he can rescue us in all circumstances, disrupt our daily routines and demonstrate for us what His love and goodness look like; making us witnesses that He loves and cares for you and me!

Have you recently been disrupted by Jesus' saving power. Go on share your living testimony with us!

"I pray that out of His glorious riches he may strengthen you with power through His Spirit in your inner being, so that Christ may dwell in your hearts through faith, And I pray that you being rooted, and established in love, may have power, together with all saints, to grasp how wide and long and high and deep is the love of Christ, And to know that this love that surpasses knowledge- that you may be filled to the measure of fullness of God. Now to Him who is able to do immeasurably more than all we ask or imagine, according to His power that is at work within us; to Him be glory in the church and in Christ Jesus throughout all generations, for ever and ever! Amen"

Ephesians 3:16–21

Have a blessed day!

LIVING WATERS

"Whoever believes in me, as the Scripture has said, streams of living water will flow from within him"

John 7:38

Today I received marching orders; no I had not been terminated yet, but felt as though I had better respond quickly to an e-mail request that beckoned for my immediate attention. Admittedly I was not in the mood, but I respectfully answered the questions via e-mail. I had just marched from the break room, ice water in hand and relieved I could now move on to another task. Moments ago I had responded to an e-mail that took longer than I anticipated. In my response I wanted to be courteous, but I just wanted it over. My brief note took on the appearance of a business letter, if only I had been able to address the person face-to-face or even by phone, this exercise could have been halted.

You cannot convince me that electronic mail is not a device used by many whom simply rather duck and hide behind their computers in the guise of *I am too busy to talk with you.* It's the perfect tool for those in the office that prefer not to stop and talk to their co-workers. The joy of conversing is so foreign in the business world. "Net" communication has taken on a new meaning. Computers have catapulted us into a more isolated society. Once upon a time you got out of your seat to speak with a coworker. Now you might phone them and say, "Hey you didn't respond to my e-mail." Did you know that there is now something called e-mail etiquette? There's a long list of don'ts, so no one is offended. Imagine that.

But on the other hand I do appreciate the efficiency of electronic mail. It is an ingenious invention for this decade. E-mail allows you to transact business in a split second, send correspondences to friends and family in faraway places and forward documentation in seconds. So just possibly I need to lighten up on the e-mail soapbox. Okay, I'll step down now.

This it is what I really was urged to share with you, that God will use our frustrations as personal teaching moments. Often it's not till later that what we have is what Oprah calls "Aha Moments." Remember when I marched back to my desk with ice water in hand? My thoughts were consumed with how much of my time had been taken addressing something I wasn't in the mood for. At that split second as I reached for my ice water, the cup jumped out of my hand. I loudly gasped, but remained cool, so that I not bring too much attention to myself. Remember my cubical is so small, that any private moments or unusual sounds are heard by the world. I was too embarrassed to put out an SOS. The main pool of water rushed towards the keyboard. If I didn't stop this water flow my system, would have been destroyed, I didn't want to think about it. In sight there was not a paper towel, napkin nothing to absorb the water. There to my surprise I had spotted a plastic bag, which the cleansers mistakenly left. It was too far to reach, but I leaped as though I was in a marathon. Frantically I placed a plastic bag over the water and now melting ice cubes. I was angry at first, before I realized it, I said out loud, "No you don't devil." I then began to laugh. This was what living water does, move swiftly, assuredly, and none stop.

This water was moving at unbelievable speed. I scooped up my Bible, moved the Rolodex of phone numbers, dictionary and grabbed some tissues I discovered in the back of my drawer. I tried to stop the uncooperative fluid. I could not hinder the water from drenching and seeping under my glass desk cover. My favorite photos, e-mail addresses written on sticky notes, scriptures that divert me from the office hubbub, and post cards with art that I dearly would love to have hanging on my wall had all been affected by my cup of *living water*. I placed all my wet items out to dry, the paper began to curl on the edges but my favorite things were salvaged. Now they just needed to dry out!

God's word is so rich, of course you realize that I read John 7 this morning:

> "Whoever believes in me, as the Scripture has said, streams of living water will flow from within him."
>
> John 7:38

I understand that through this spilled water, I am to relay to you the power of the living water that is provided to us as believers in Christ Jesus. We have access to life giving and life changing water.

The water is the word and the power of the Holy Ghost. It cannot be hindered or stopped. It's much like my spill this morning, I couldn't react fast enough to stop what was inevitable—the flow would reach under my desktop protector and could not be ignored. God's real life analogies are truly something to marvel at.

I know you realize friends; it was no happenstance that I read in the *African-American Devotional Bible*, John 7, and review the commentary *Living Water* by Reverend Dr. Alicia D. Byrd, and spill water this day. This water represents how swiftly God's word can transform our lives. This living water affects us profoundly, spurs positive change, and makes you wonder why you took so long to drink from this refreshing nectar. A cloud begins to lift over our lives, miracles occur and God's living water ebbs and flows throughout our lives.

So friends should you spill your water, have some setbacks, it's not the end for us. There's enough living water for all of us;

simply open your Holy Bibles read, believe and be assured that God's word is sustaining and life changing. Please join me in this prayer:

> *Jesus, Christ, sweet Lamb of God we thank you today for the assurance that your living water is real and no matter what our life circumstances. Good can come from broken lives. You have instructed us in your word and with Your Holy Spirit. We can face tomorrow because You are always there. We believe, You are a present help and we simply need to open up our hearts and invite you to come in. We pray that your living water will wash over us, keep us, restore us, and establish us. Lord we thank you! There is no other as wonderful as You! We praise your Holy name. Amen.*

Making My Appeal

"Because he loves me, says the Lord, I will rescue him;
I will protect him; for he acknowledges my name."

Psalm 91:14

Friends, I could not rest until I shared this with you today. Today was my appeal date for contesting the decision of my not receiving unemployment. My appointment was scheduled for 2 p.m. I did not have a fleet of high-powered attorneys and a briefcase loaded with convincing evidence. I simply had my story, my testimony and I was making an appeal, an appeal to turn the decision around and send me my unemployment.

You do know anxiety and stress make you tired?

Pushing myself to do some household chore seemed to be the answer. I really had no intention of washing three loads of clothes, but I did. I pulled the bin of dirty clothing down the stairs and got to work. I then returned to the girls' bedrooms, dragging into plain sight dirty clothes, crumpled up papers, rollers and markers and whatever else was hiding under beds. Then I found a garbage bag to collect the hidden piles. Normally I would have left the piles for the owners to see and throw away. Why I think the perpetrators will be convicted of this behavior and stop is beyond me. Children do not see what parents see. Realizing this I was in no mood for that exercise of finger pointing and instead picked up the miscellaneous pile of loot and placed the bag on the doorknob, they can discard the bag later.

What I was really doing was not focusing on my impending appeal. Then I stopped, sat down, got still, listened to the house's silence and the tears flowed. I was sad. I wanted to speak with my mother.

Mothers, or those we think of as surrogate mamas, have a way of soothing and comforting us. Mamas can get to the heart of the matter, they cut to the chase. My need was immediate; the thought was pushed aside for a moment not to bother her, not to upset her with my concern. But I am sure the Holy Spirit fought with my reservations about sharing with her that I needed her and her prayers. I made the long distant call anyhow.

Oh, there was her voice, good medicine, and my eyes began to well up. Although she was in Buffalo for a split second I felt as though she was standing in Norfolk, in my family room and hugging me. She was preparing to go to the doctor because she was bothered with pink eye. My heart went out to her. She didn't need the irritation of pink eye and not feeling good on top of that. Mom has degenerative arthritis. My concerns then began to trickle out in between my tears. I really wanted her to pray for me. She said she would, but said the most important prayer is the one I would say on my behalf. She said she would phone me later. I felt better.

Friends, as I reflect God knew of my pending appeal. There were no legal eagles as my entourage, but the Holy Ghost was present and would be there with me through this experience. The scripture reassured us that:

"If you make the Most High your dwelling-even the Lord, who is my refuge-then no harm will befall you, no disaster will come near your tent. For he will command his angels concerning you to guard you in all your ways; they will lift you up in their hands, so that you will not strike your foot against a stone"

Psalm 91:9–12

God was fully aware of my need to hear an encouraging word.

Thank you daddy! Thank you! He was present, with me, when I listened to the silence and wept like a baby. The phone rang, and it was our mother friend, Sister Josephine who lives not far from me, her words were sent from the throne room.

Linda, I've been praying for you, be sure to read Psalm 91. Whatever they decide God knows what you need.

God placed it on Sister Josephine's heart to call me. I thanked God for her words, took a nap, felt refreshed and was ready for the appeal hearing.

Before leaving home I did just that, read Psalm 91. Those words blessed me and breathed life into me. Our Heavenly Father was speaking and appealing to me now that I was under His protection, and He is my defender and protector.

I remember hearing another mother /friend, Evangelist Wilma Taylor says when you are reading the scripture insert your name in the appropriate places in the text.

Evangelist Wilma Taylor helped me to understand that the scripture is appealing to my need and I have the authority to apply it to me and what concerns me. Friends let me suggest a technique that you begin to use when reading your Holy Scripture; begin to personalize the scripture by inserting your name when you read the words 'they', 'those', and 'you'. You will begin to have a new ownership and a deeper love for God's word as it resonates into your spirit that this was written with you in mind! Psalm 91:14 will have new meaning!

"Because [Linda] loves me," says the Lord, "I will rescue [Linda]; I will protect [her], for [she] acknowledges my name. [She] will call upon me, and I will answer [her]; I will be with [her] in trouble, I will deliver [her] and honor [her]. With long life I will satisfy [Linda] and shows [her] my salvation."

One Foot In Front
of The Other

"...For the Lord your God is gracious and compassionate. He will not turn his face from you, if you return to him."

2 Chronicles 30:9

It was as though I was looking at the Haiti pictures for the first time. It had not mattered that I had seen them at least a dozen times. Some of these pictures were at least ten years old; they would seem to crop up in a pile of mail. Later I'd see them in the corner in my photo basket and now here they were again, making a reappearance scattered on the desk, our desk at home where we work on the computer, I write my devotionals and occasionally play electronic Scrabble.

So, today this was no accident that before I would write this devotional I would again see my husband surrounded with his Haitian friends in a church without stained glass windows, designated seating for the dignitaries and a communion table. Instead this church was packed with men and women kneeling on the dirt carpeted floor, their arms extended in the air, mouths open and unashamedly praising God. During this same excursion there were more pictures of my husband assembled with men who were clad in crisp clean shirts and ties. They all appeared very official. Some of these dignified men were standing with students in schoolhouses, others were standing against aluminum sided dwellings and yet others standing on unpaved roads.

There was no mistaking that they were in a tropical paradise, where the standard of living was quiet different from what most of us are accustomed to. Yes this was a tropical paradise, with no indication of leisure and wealth; instead there was a sea of hard working men, women and studious children who often lived from day to day with one foot in front of the other. Many of their faces appeared to be worn, dusty and tired. They smile through the hardship, but they love Jesus and would travel for miles to hear the good news.

These photos are part of my home's décor and I believe this is on purpose. I do believe my husband enjoys having them out as reminders about how simple and uncomplicated our lives can be. Also they are wonderful reminders of the need that exists in the world, the world that's not so very far from ours. A world that might not have as many strip malls, fast food restaurants and grocery stores as we are accustomed to.

Last month my husband and several other missionaries were blessed with being able to travel to South Africa, there again was that resounding theme.

The theme seems to be that if we Christians can just persevere—just push and hold out and on to hope that deliverance is on the way. I am sure that's what the Holy Spirit is instructing us to do. God wants us to believe that today friends. God realizes that we too have hopes and dreams like our Christian brothers and sisters throughout the world.

One foot in front of the other is our universal march!

> "For I know the plans I have for you, declares the Lord, plans to prosper you and not harm you, plans to give you hope and a future."
>
> Jeremiah 29:11

These Christians in Zambia, like in Haiti are rich with cultural pride and spiritual beliefs. They are challenged by famine, poverty, and government restrictions. They are seeking answers and requesting relief from stretching merger wages and diminishing food and medical supplies. They are looking to other Christians for assistance in their social and economic plights, holding fast to prayers that solicit God's benevolence through your generosity that will ease the burden and load they carry as they move one foot in front of the other.

As I looked at the pictures, I felt this wonderful connection, I too am now eager to meet my brothers and sister in Christ who live abroad. They are prayerful and so full of hope. Hope for a better tomorrow for their communities, school houses, and churches that will draw others to Jesus. They hope for desks, French and English textbooks, sewing machines, and salaries of $5. and $10. to pay their minister's and teacher's monthly wages. They hope for bibles and good crops that will yield a decent wage. They hope that you will have a heart and learn of their need and compassionately give.

Until we meet our Haitian and Zambian Christian brothers and sisters, let's remember that that we too can ask:

> "…The priests and the Levites stood to bless the people, and God heard them, for their prayer reached heaven, his holy dwelling place."

2 Chronicles 30:27

In his home in heaven God will hear our prayers and accept them…Yes, we can ask God to lead us to an established missions organization, entreat our friends and congregations to rally around and support mission efforts to build up our brothers and sisters in foreign lands. We can learn from missionaries first hand what the people say their needs are and seed into that ministry of need. Surely, it's just that simple—realistically we will not all travel abroad, but our impact can be as powerful and those who travel on the field.

Friends, we too can place one foot in front of the other in our efforts of demonstrating a Jesus kind of love!!

Carry on missionaries and have a blessed morning.

POURED OUT LIKE
A DRINK OFFERING

"As you hold out the word of life-in order that I may boast on the day of Christ that I did not run or labor for nothing. But even if I am being poured out like a drink offering on the sacrifice and service coming from your faith, I am glad and rejoice with all of you."

Philippians 2:16–17

Even me Lord, Bless me, Even me

Those were the words Yolanda Adams sang as tears streamed down my cheeks. There I sat in my mother's comfortable home, her worn chair that provided so many memories. All I could do was try not to holler, yes! And yell out. I didn't want to startle mama, alarm her. But my heart was so heavy and I too was tired. Yolanda Adams was singing my song, a song that spoke of needing to be blessed and not overlooked, not forsaken.

These past days had been just what the doctor ordered. My friends had come to Norfolk and rescued me. They and my husband insisted that I needed to go back to Buffalo and get away from my home that seemed to lately not feel like my safety zone, but instead a turbulent storm and war zone. There was indeed a spiritual war going on and I suffered from battle fatigue. My stepchildren were now home with us, no matter how temporary, they were alive and present and it seemed that the confusion was mounting and my husband's eyes appeared to be open but whenever I voiced a concern, his eyes were open shut! Yes and so our conversations became accusations and indictments, seeming a never ending flow of hurtful words, our words that now cut and left deep gashes. We were both living outside of our usually loving character.

I needed respite, refuge and there I sat in my mother's second bedroom with over stuffed luggage. Thursday I'd be returning home and I wasn't ready under the present circumstances. I didn't want to leave my mother; it was safe and peaceful by her side. She often feeling lonely and was suffering from debilitating arthritis. It was apparent that my visit was good medicine. She said so. She needed me and I needed her. Going back to Norfolk was where I now resided, but I didn't feel like being poured out like a drink offering any longer. I loved Norfolk, my college community; our present home represented hope and God's evident love in our life. My sacred place, my praying space, my sanctuary now was filled with a confusing atmosphere that overwhelmed and angered me. I wanted my peace back, my sweet flow of things, but everything had abruptly seemed to change and I felt powerless to adequately handle this like I wanted.

Lately my spiritual walk seemed more like a limp and a stagger, not a victorious strut! I dare not utter this in my prayers:

God, how could this be? But you know it was in my spirit, friends! Has this ever been in your spirit?

What was happening? And then Yolanda Adams sang: "*Bless me, Protect me, Help me, Yes, even me!*"

As Yolanda was singing my song, my soul was lamenting just that. And then I opened my bible to the book of Philippians not really seeking answers.

Friends, I was just compelled to do this. I knew God wanted me to understand that I needed to imitate Christ's humanity. Was I ready for that? No way was this the answer I desired. How could God do this to me? Oh, but friends He had a greater purpose in mind. You probably see it already.

Please read Philippians Chapter 2 for yourself. God desires

that all of us move from selfish motives and embrace a state of humility and consciously consider others; this moves us to greater capacity to love others-love our husbands who are not perfect, and not always able to see with our eyes. The Holy Spirit just said that often the unlovable behavior that the stepchildren exhibit is for our eyes only, and we stepparents must know that often children are acting out of their feelings of bewilderment and anxiety. They're confused and we are too. Feelings of being unworthy, unloved, unaccepted and unappreciated are powerful emotions that many carry around. Just possibly these children need the love and attention that only we can offer. Lord why does it have to be such a struggle?

Too bad step-parents don't have a little manual with specific *how-to's* on days when we are stretched thin and poured out like a drink offering! You are absolutely correct we do have a manual—the Holy Bible it's for everyone and anyone seeking guidance.

Now friends I am not excusing the children's disrespectful behavior, the talking back, and the suggestive body language that say's everything but you know! But in spite of that God's word says that I must adapt and conform my attitude to be the same as Jesus Christ.

> "Who, being in the very nature God, did not consider equality with God something to be grasped, but made himself nothing, taking the very nature of a servant, being made in human likeness"
>
> Philippians 2:6,7

Yolanda Adams hasn't stopped singing yet; she is further encouraging us to:

"Remember the Lord is with us, Tell him how much you need Him. He's got your miracle. Give your impossibilities to Jesus. It's

gonna be alright. Give your impossibilities to Jesus. Your miracle is on the way!"

Do you know that Jesus is your secret place? When your friends can't come and rescue you, when you're out of arm reach of loved ones, get to your secret place quick-the comforting words of God, pick up your Holy Bible. My visit back home was purposed for my needed time of rest and renewal. Buffalo was figuratively the secret place that connected me again with our loving Heavenly Father. In Buffalo, at my mama's house I had an opportunity to peacefully read my Holy Bible and hear from God.

God words are conveying to all of us that we must expand our capacity to love those that don't know how to love us. This can only be done supernaturally. In our fragile step parenting and natural parenting states it's nearly impossible on a natural level.

I know that God will have to show me how to speak with out straining and to stop yelling and scolding in a shrill voice. He'll have to show me how to discern the important from the unimportant and give me His wisdom to step up and confront without fear. I don't intend to be a martyr; I just want to do this God's way.

God is awaiting us friends to seek and ask him for instructions on how to renew our strength, give over ourselves to him, and hold on to Jesus Christ our Lord and Savior for dear life. Can't you just see Him taking our hand and holding us up while we consider other's welfare, embrace unselfishness, humility and strive for holy ambition?

We might be poured out from life's upsets and suffering from burnout, but I now realize that the Almighty:

> "As we draw closer to God, He unearths spiritual jewels that are hidden deep with in us. Embracing unselfishness, humility and consideration for the welfare of

others empties us of ourselves and makes us vessels for God's use by expanding our capacity to love. When we are filled up with Christ, we are able to manifest the kingdom of God on earth." (Bennett, 1280)

The God we serve has given us the holy one, who has poured new life, new hopes and new strength and vitality into me and yes, you too—only if we believe!

Have a blessed day!

Reminded & Renewed

"I long to dwell in your tent forever and take refuge in the shelter of your wings…"

Psalms 61:4

As I inserted my key in the locked back door, I began to wonder if it was Miss Maime or her chair, which brings me so much comfort. At this given moment I am not quite sure?

I am sure that you too have similar experiences when you visit your favorite barber or beautician. I have witnessed men in the barber's chair; whether there's a crowd or not, there's always a stimulating conversation and then the conversation takes an abrupt turn for a more deep and meaningful exchange. Surprisingly, a real exchange on a personal level is birthed. You can sense it in the air that the conversation wasn't supposed to be so passionate.

So you understand what I am referring to, as you slide into the chair and the technician in my case is Miss Maime who perfectly adjusts the chair for the work that's about to occur.

You know it's your turn. She glances at you, smiles and then say's, *Come on I don't want to keep you waiting.* The feeling of relief gives in and you just want to holler "Uncle" as though you were in a headlock. Before the chair is warm, out spills discussions, deep discussions on topics you don't normally share with just anyone.

What am I speaking about friends? There's scripture to back it up, see if you can't find it?

"….For out of the overflow of the heart the mouth speaks"

Oh don't kid me; it's some of the most therapeutic work we can experience. This therapy can filter through distracting noises, heat, chemicals, and personalities. Judge Judy can't even disturb an engaging exchange.

It's reassuring that standing behind you is an attentive, listening, caring person. Ms. Maime is that for me. She's my hairdresser, but she's my confidante, my friend, she's a loving, genuine mother figure. I feel absolutely at peace when I enter her doors. Her shop is in her home, smack dab in the middle of her kitchen floor. (Aren't kitchens always inviting?) Her home is conveniently located so that you're not traveling a million miles out of the way to be shampooed and sat in a corner until the fifty women in front of you are blow-dried, colored, cut and permed. No not at Miss Maime's.

God knows I am grateful for her sanctuary and her Godly wisdom and prayers. Yes, we agree to pray for each other. I am reminded and renewed!

There's order and Maime has it down to a science. Should you come a little late she doesn't fuss or make you feel awkward. She gingerly continues working with the customer in front of you, stops after she has conditioned or rolled them and then you are given the kid glove treatment.

This almost sounds as though I am promoting her business. No I am sharing with you about her love and her consideration for those that she serves. Do her character traits remind you of anyone?

Honestly, whether I give you the prices and locations that does not matter. Her clientele gives referrals and she's not hurting for business. The Holy Spirit has drawn a perfect parallel for us. We can experience Maime's love and have direct access to our

Heavenly Father's never ending supply of love. Just as I weekly go to Ms. Maime and am renewed and restored as I sit in her chair and it seems a floodgate of concerns, aspirations, and hopes just pour out of me. I can go directly to Jesus and tell Him all about it!

Tonight I announced, "I'm fine till I get here and then I just feel like I want to cry." *(*The truth is I want to cry because I can cry and not be judged. After I cry, I am comforted.)

Maime was taken a back and said, "Why? I hope I don't depress you."

Quite the contrary! I thought.

God would have it on the days when my personal challenges are more than I can bare up under, I can make my way to a place, a physical place and receive spiritual renewal and personal restoration.

How blessed are we to have earthly accommodations for spiritual sustenance. Well friends you too are blessed to be able to have heavenly experiences in the midst of earthly challenges. We can experience the love of Christ Jesus in our blessed encounters. He's beckoning you to come and sit at His feet and share all of your hearts concerns, your defeats, your worries, your unspoken anxieties and most certainly your thanksgivings. So if you can't hold it until your next barber or beautician's visit, Jesus is a prayer away.

> "Hear my cry, O God; listen to my prayer. From the ends of the earth I call to you, I call as my heart grows faint ; lead me to the rock that is higher than I."
>
> Psalm 61:1–2

Good Morning!

A Solemn Vow of Hope

"It was revealed to them that they were not serving themselves but you, when they spoke of the things that have now been told you by those who have preached the gospel to you by the Holy Spirit sent from heaven. Even angels long to look into these things."

1 Peter 1:12

I want to be in partnership with God. Let me establish this from the onset. Does it sound as though I have an air of haughtiness? Please forgive me if it sounds as though I am being sanctimonious, I am just making a declaration, mostly speaking out loud to myself. It's time I made a solemn vow to the Lord and kept it.

You do realize that sometimes your beliefs don't sink in, don't take hold, don't take root in your spirit until you speak *it;* say *it* bluntly and out loud.

I earnestly believe this devotional is more for me than you today, but I do like sharing. Just recently I silently made several vows to my self. No way would I experience *this* again at age forty-six! This meaning so much of life's set backs and heart aches. Who am I kidding? No way do I have a handle on that! But yes, indeed, I can choose to make some life changing choices.

Today as I stood at my kitchen sink, washed the few dishes and began prepping for my Sunday dinner. I spoke out loud, statements that were contrary to what was really going through my mind. Statements that went something like:

God is here with me and He'll continue to be with me.
My next job will be a rewarding job, I've blessed others
on the job and will do so on the next. I know who God is

and His provision has not left me lacking. My testimonies
have drawn others to the Kingdom I will not be afraid to
honestly share my trails. I do want to publish them and I
will publish them! God has good things in store for me. It
appears to be bleak, but that's the furthest thing from the
truth. My marriage is built on a sure foundation.

For approximately two weeks I have been holding down the household responsibilities while my son has been at a summer educational program and my husband out of the country on a Missions trip. During their absence, several weeks ago I received my own news flash and knew I needed a break from the day-to-day drudgery of household responsibilities. I too must take time for myself, but my excuse has been it's never in the budget. Honestly, it has been anything but delightful, since my husband went to Africa. I have had lots of time to think.

I have been bombarded with disappointments on top of disappointments. The silence in my home is usually comforting, a calming space, but instead the quiet, stillness seemed to help push me in the realization that these rough time were unsettling for me.

The assuredness of respite in between jobs seemed to be dashed. This respite was unwelcome. My hope dissipated when I was informed that I did not qualify for unemployment. Just this past Friday, I was prompted by a friend to contest this decision. The appeal process was easier than I imagined. So the benefits determination status is on hold until my hearing. My focus had now been sifted to *next-steps* because unemployment benefits have been denied. Instead of contemplating visits with my family in Georgia and seeing Mama, "things are back to square one and I am at a financial standstill. I need a new direction or course of action, now!

"What am I going to do?" Well you ask an important question! My prayers haven't halted the US Postal delivery of urgent notices, shut off notices, and monthly statements.

In my despair, I have cried a river tears. I too know what Langston Hughes is speaking about. You are thinking, not you, not possibly now? Yes me; yesterday, last week and during this writing. In between the crying I am constantly reading uplifting bible verses, challenging spiritual commentaries and sending prayers up that I know touch the heart of God. But admittedly, when my view is clouded, I soon sink back into the reality that something needs to change.

Good news change is on the way!

Today, I made my bold auditory statements. Yes I did, I stood at my kitchen sink, hands in the dishwater, and I pronounced life into a dying situation. I am sure God prompted this because mentally I was not in a positive frame of mind. No way was this a planned undertaking on my part.

The enemy wants me to feel angry, tired, challenged, abandoned and hopeless. I would like to think that my Sovereign Father said, *let me quickly see about my child. She needs me.*

Call on him friends. Call God for His help now. I assure you He will answer.

"We are hard pressed on every side, but not crushed; perplexed, but not in despair; persecuted, but not abandoned; struck down, but not destroyed. We always carry around in our body the death of Jesus, so that the life of Jesus may also be revealed in our body. For we who are alive are always being given over to death for Jesus' sake, so that his life may be revealed in our mortal body."

2 Corinthians 4:8–12

And there I stood alone in my kitchen and vowed my life would not come crumbling down. At the time I didn't exactly understand it that way. I just needed to feel better and as I spoke positively, the negative reality was overshadowed. God and a host of angels were my witnesses.

Earlier that morning they heard me say, "I don't want these trials and hardships any more. God this is too much!" I spoke out of my pain. After I uttered all of that, I asked God to please forgive me.

As I write this devotional it becomes clearer to me that as I spoke in the kitchen,

- *I needed to hold onto HOPE.*
- *HOPE in an everlasting Heavenly Father.*
- *HOPE that if the bills didn't stop coming that I would change my perspective.*
- *HOPE that I would not buckle under the pressure.*
- *HOPE that I would not make mockery of my faith, writing one thing, stating another and thinking yet another.*

Remember I shared with you that I have had so much time to reflect and read? One of the absolute jewels in our library is a book entitled, *Hope Again When Life Hurts and Dreams Fade,* by Charles R. Swindoll.

Never before this time had I paid much attention to this book. During one of those lonely moments I reached towards my bookcase scanned the title and there it was.

Mr. Swindoll helped me to understand my current state of "hard times." He did not mix words or dress up what so many of us are currently experiencing. Thank you, Holy Spirit, for his chapter, "Rejoicing Through Hard Times." As I read, I knew God had an encouraging message for me. Let me share it with you. I instantly understood that what was missing for me during these rough times was some jubilance, some heartfelt *joy!*

No I am not kidding you. The missing link has been an absence of a spirit of rejoicing, establishing in my self the truth that:

> "Blessed be the God and Father of our Lord Jesus Christ, who according to His great mercy has caused us to obtain an inheritance which is imperishable and undefiled and will not fade away, reserved in heaven for you."

> I Peter 1:3–4

So there it is friends, we have a hope beyond our suffering. In Chuck Swindoll's words:

> "How can we rejoice through our pain? How can we have hope beyond our suffering? Because we have a living hope, we have a permanent inheritance, we have a divine protection, we have a developing faith, we have an unseen Savior, and we have a guaranteed deliverance."

Glory to God! Why don't you embrace this solemn vow with me? *Lord, Jesus Christ, our Savior and our friend, I promise never to forget who I am in you and the eternal hope that belongs to me, no matter the suffering or pain! I will rejoice in your goodness!*

Hold on to hope friends have a super day!

So Much to
Thank Him For

"Our mouths were filled with laughter, our tongues
with songs of joy .Then it was said among the nations,
The Lord has done great things for them."

Psalm 126:2–3

God, do you know that I am here? Of course you do. But lately I've been hard pressed to remember to marvel at God's glory over the heads of my stepchildren. I don't always feel blessed in this regard. Often it has felt and been so much! So much more responsibility for me, more required love and tolerance on my part than I felt was measured out to me. I always envisioned I would love more children, call those I hadn't birthed mine. But the here and now is a harsher reality than I imagined, yet I must remain thankful, I am a blessed woman.

I knew that when I returned home this morning from running errands and dropping kids off for band that my stepson would be perched on the coach enjoying NFL highlights. Well I wasn't disappointed and I am sure my stepson was in football heaven. The players were huddled together, the sports commentator was on top of his job and then there it was, the play was being executed, the fans were cheering and the volume on the television was blaring. I tried to ignore this, but whom was I really kidding. I didn't want to feel as though I was in some sports arena this morning. No I was in my family room, I was at home.

Then I thought to myself, *Nope this is too early for this and I refuse too ask what are your plans for today?* But I did remind him of the two chores I asked him to take care of yesterday. He removed himself from the coach and without a word began to do them. I tell this because I am not trying to paint any picture other than what I am seeing. But there's so much more to the picture and you know that's the truth.

My stepson is a young man that's very endearing, there's noting vindictive about him. I just wish he knew that life awaits him. That is so much more than mediocre. He's a young man that is passionate about football, music, and history. If you saw him you'd wonder why he wasn't somebody's line backer, tackler, or some powerhouse executing self-fulfilling decisions on or off the field. I purposely turned the channel and listened to Gospel music on the Music Choice station. That was a better alternative to asking him what his plans are for the day.

Do you know that God encourages us through others words? Well this morning He's done that especially with lyrics and music of the song entitled: "So Much."

So much, so much to thank God for. I thank Him for my mind, My health and strength. For everything He's made. So much to thank Him for.

"Thank Him Song." by Michael Brooks, Album:
Choice To Rejoice.

I am sure there are more lyrics but essentially the song is a reminder that there's so much to be thankful for that we shouldn't become despondent or afraid. Can't you just hear your song, the song that ministers to you and speaks to your heart, the song with the distinct cords, beats, and tempo? It's anointed music that ignites a wellspring of hidden and denied emotions. God is tugging on our heart when that occurs.

He has a divine message just for us today. Just as I could not ignore the football stadium effect in my family room and I could not ignore the simple, but profound message this morning!

Friends I like you don't always shift my focus from the pain, hurt, and emotional weights that spiritually deplete us and over-shadow the gratitude that we should have so much of.

That message friends is, if only we realize that we have so much to be thankful for, just possibly our outlook and our actions would reflect that. This morning I am going to take my own medicine and deliberately not allow the enemy to play field hockey in my head with promoting negative thoughts. *It is so!*

I have stopped asking questions to what I already know the answers to. Instead I am now praying and believing Jesus for so much more power in my family's lives, so much more love for all of us to experience, greater good for all of us, especially my step-children. I am no longer asking God why and being impatient! Instead I choose to thank God so much, for so Much!!

I want to challenge you friends to change your spiritual sta-tions and begin fresh, right this moment to *expect so much, believe so much, and thank our Heavenly Father so much* for the great good that you currently are experiencing and the great good that is about to burst forth.

Have a blessed day!

A THOUSAND STORIES

"For wisdom will enter your heart, and knowledge will be pleasant to your soul. Discretion will protect you, and understanding will guard you."

Proverbs 2:10–11

Today, I had wisdom enough to understand that I too had learned so much from my stories and many other life lessons, but I also had wisdom enough to know there was so much more in store to learn.

Thinking that I would just relax, drink a cup of tea and wind down; I headed for the coach and then clicked on the jazz music station, playing was a wonderfully mellow composition entitled, Thousand Stories, the artist was, Turning Point. Aren't they creative and wasn't this divine timing again? Then a mental strobe light clicked on and signaled my brain to give me snapshots and in some instances panoramic views of my life and the turning points that would set my spiritual journey reeling.

Authors like J. California Cooper, Dorothy West and Zora Neal Hurston know how to tell a story and show you yourself through their characters that draw you in and invariably compel you to write and live your story.

We all have a testimony, a current trial, several tests, and many stories that speak to the roads we have traveled in our lives. How many stories do you have? Stories that tell of your life, your hearts desire, your deep passions, your victories, your near accomplishments and yes, disappointments?

After you told your stories did you who reflect with wisdom what your lessons taught you? Did you learn and then realize that there was a turning point.

I remember listening to my father, John, speak about his father, Joseph and the journeys he took from Florida that lead him to Buffalo, New York to marry my grandmother Rita and raise three children in a neighborhood that was predominantly Italian. Now there was a story. Joseph Mose, Sr. was much like many young men living in the late 1930's and 1940's in the South lured North by the promise of less field labor and more employment opportunities in steel plants and other factories. My grandfather and his contemporaries responded to the call seeking capable, young, strong men hoping and dreaming about securing a bigger piece of the American pie. I would like to think that my grandfather viewed this pie as more than just ownership of an automobile and a home with a white picket fence. His dream encompassed making a difference for his sister Mattie, a future wife and family. My grandfather Joe's dreams carved out stories that desired to create a world that provided improved social, economic and spiritual prosperity. He dreamed a world that I could walk around in several generations later, free to make choices and live abundantly.

American poet Langston Hughes echoes this sentiment in his poem:

"I Dream a World":

"I dream a world where man no other man will scorn, Where love will bless the earth and peace its path adorn. I dream a world where all Will know sweet freedoms way, Where greed no longer saps the soul. Nor avarice blights our day. A world I dream where black or white, Whatever race you be, Will share the bounties of the earth and every man is free, Where wretchedness will hang its head and joy, like a pearl, attends the needs of all mankind of such I dream, my world! My families' stories all have a resounding theme and that is: No matter what try's to get in our way we will win! They tightly gripped their dreams and were determined to follow them."

When I traveled with my grandfather Ellsworth down back roads in Gaithersburg and Darnestown, I listened intently as he reminisced with his childhood friends and elderly cousins what growing up was like for them in Maryland. Grand pop fondly spoke of his father, William "Papa" Jackson and mother, Hattie.

William Jackson was fiercely devoted to his family. He like Joseph Mose, Sr. had a vision, mission and dream for his family. His story would take him away from his family during the week to be a landscaper at Walter Reed Hospital in Washington, D.C.

I learned more about my great grandfather William from a hand written letter in pencil dated May 13, 1936 to great grandmother Hattie. (My mother gave me this priceless gift; her mother gave it to her!) It gives me glimpse of what life was like for my great grandfather and how conscientious he was about the health and welfare of his loved ones. My mother proudly displays his picture. He was small in stature, but from the many family stories he was big in character. William Jackson was also a loving man of great faith and a minister of the Gospel that offered hope. He demonstrated his love by caring for the sick and being generous to those in need. Apparently there were limited jobs for men in Darnestown. He would do like many other men and women would who wanted to support their families—he would leave his family during the week and travel miles away to Washington, D.C. His proficient gardening abilities help feed them in his absence. His pride was shown in his work as a meticulous landscaper. I am not sure about his formal education, but if his letters are any indication of his brilliance, he was also very wise. Unfortunately my great grandfather suffered a stroke and died in the heat of the day doing his job on the grounds of the Walter Reed Hospital.

It was nothing but sheer faith in God that encouraged my ancestors to travel miles away from their families often to face obstacles of racism, financial strain, poor health and countless turns of adverse circumstances that challenged their humanity. But thank God that was not the end of their story. My great grandfather Joseph's lineage continues. How do I know? My father is alive, my brothers and their children, my first cousins and their children. Why we are the hope and dreams of our ancestors. (Find Maya Angelou's poem, "And Still I Rise." That's our story.) And yes, our living hope is in Christ Jesus. I, like you, am still here pushing and believing God as we tell our story during this faith journey.

Friends let me encourage you to know that you too are the living proof of your ancestor's faith. We are here alive with God's promise. Our story will be the next generation's story. What have you chosen to write in your life's book for your loved ones encouragement? I would like to think that if we are grounded in faith our living legacy is an important chapter for all who desire to listen to learn how we carved out our way in this world.

My bible tells me and you that we are "fearfully and wonderfully made." Find it in your concordance friends and commit it to memory. I believe that God has encouraged us this day as we, access our Lord and Savior, Jesus Christ to help us with our many stories.

"Therefore, having been justified by faith, we have peace with God through our Lord Jesus Christ, through whom also we have access by faith into this grace in which we stand, and rejoice in hope of the glory of God. And not only that, but we also glory

in tribulations, knowing that tribulation produces perseverance; and perseverance, character; and character;
hope."

Romans 5:1–4

Have a blessed day!

We Shall
Behold Him

"She will give birth to a son, and you are to give him
the name Jesus, because he will save his people from
their sins. All this took place to fulfill what the Lord
had said through the prophet: The virgin will be with
child and will give birth to a son, and they will call him
Immanuel-which means, God with us"

Matthew1: 21–23

God is with us, all the time. Yes, it's true it's a fact, even
when our home lives are turning upside down. I long to
rise in the arms of faith and draw nearer to the Lord and I am
convinced that God is using my stepchildren to convict me of
the need to trust and rely on Him/ Emmanuel totally. Let me try
and explain.

I had just awakened from a much-needed nap and began
reflecting on what an exceptional day this had been! My home
had been blessed and graced with the presence our dear friend
and pastor from Buffalo, Bishop Dwight Brown. My heart could
not contain the joy with the thought that earlier there sat Bishop
Brown in Norfolk, Virginia at my dining room table, enjoying
a fish fry (which he provided) and then retreated to our living
room—just visiting, just looking like his wonderfully blessed self,
just reflecting, and just making us feel all so at ease with his genuine warmth.

God knew our household needed his visit, this day! Bishop
Brown is an atmosphere changer! I am sure you know many peo-

ple who are just that, atmosphere changers. They enter your presence and your life and worlds are never quite the same.

That's just what I was reflecting on, how my family and friends whom sat in the presence of our beloved friend were at peace and comforted by his presence.

His visit was much to short. Bishop Brown was then whisked off to return to his private sanctuary and our home was back in its full momentum.

Thank You Lord with sweet glimpses and the manifestation of your word!

Friends did you realize that we behold Jesus over and over again when we least expect it? How many times my husband and I had spoken to our spiritual advisor, our Pastor and friend in confidence, shared joys and concerns with him over the phone; long distance was generally our method of communication and now, there he sat, in the flesh, live and in living color!!

Once again we were witnesses to how complete God's love is.

How often have you desired to see the face of a friend and loved one, prayed for each other and just hadn't been able to physically connect and look upon the other's face?

Well just hold on because you shall see your loved ones.

Mind you this visit came at a most stressful time in my life. My life appears to be changing right before my eyes. Sometimes it appears as though I am on the sidelines looking and not quite understanding the dynamics of what's occurring.

I needed this visit more than I care to articulate.

Our home is running over with family and friends. Lately it seems there's a never ending stream of folks walking in and out our home with a frequency that would have most folks gawking with their mouths hanging open. I am not sure if you realize that in one month's time my home has grown from three individuals to six. My three stepchildren are now living in my home. And the truth of the matter is it's not just my home, but also our home. My squatting rights are over. I now am moving over to share what I loved to consider my sacred space.

I love to think that my home is running smoothly and there is some semblance of order; all of that's questionable today!

The complexion of our space had changed; the order of our days is jumbled. Suddenly I realize that the rules for blended families aren't written, in arms reach and can be taken off a shelf and slathered on with ease. Stepparents are parents but there's a gray area that unspoken! And it's uncomfortable and can leave you perplexed and resentful if it's not handled effectively, swiftly and with prayer—lots of prayer!

For you who are in blended families, have you found your selves wondering, asking, God where are you in all of this?

If you are like me you've cried and asked Jesus to *please come on in!*

And today something was distinctly different; shoes were still not neatly lined in order, one sneaker there and another here. Towels and wash clothes weren't displayed and hung strategically; instead, there were balled-up wet wash clothes lying on the floor of the tub, with dripping water and melting soap. And I indistinctly knew that the hair care basket was out of site, half empty because the hair scrunchees were in cups that obviously some had had kool-aid in it. The decorative combs, crayons, felt markers and dirty socks were either balled up or lying in several different corners.

But today friends, I wasn't spastic about the disorder, I just went on with my Father's business and declare as folks were filing out the house this song welled up in my spirit:

We Shall Behold Him.

Don't you see it friends? Jesus had changed my atmosphere, just like Bishop Brown had. Most of the words I don't even know.

So I just hummed some, sang some and made up the words to the rest!

> "The skies shall unfold preparing His entrance. The stars shall applaud him with thunders of grace. The sweet light in His eyes shall Enhance those awaiting. Then we shall behold Him, Face to face. We shall behold Him. We shall behold Him. Face to face In all of his glory We shall behold Him. We shall behold Him Face to face Our Savior and Lord! The angels shall shout, shout of his coming. The sleeping shall rise from this slumbering place. Those who remain, Shall be changed in one moment. Then we shall be hold him. We shall behold him Face to face In all of his glory, Our Savior and Lord. The angels shall shout of his coming. I'm gonna see his face in all of his glory Our Savior and God, yes we will! My savior and Lord, We shall behold him, I can hardly wait until that great day! We shall behold him as He is!"

It's late in the evening now, and yes, I was slow to get the message today. But could it be that God wants us to get some latitude in our attitude. ("Take 6" is on the stereo now.)

I am sure the Lord is telling us that we need an atmosphere changer not only in our homes, but our hearts!

Let Him in friends! I am sure God is saying to open the doors of your heart.

Emmanuel, Mary's baby, God's divine son, our Present help in Times of Trouble EMMANUEL is in the house!! My house and yours. Yes, He's there early and He stay's late. If we can only hold fast to the realization that no matter what, no matter when God is here!!!

Come on friends let's pray for a moment:

Lord nothing is too hard or impossible for you. Your holy word, the bible convicts me to only have faith and believe. Loving difficult people is next to impossible for me. I need your help. Help in the area of remembering that you are Emmanuel, "God with us". Lord when I can't love like you desire, forgive me and let me hide in you, run for shelter and you take over and regulate my mind and heart. I am open to your will and way. The safest place is with you. Thank you Jesus!

Have a blessed day!

JOY

"How awesome is the Lord Most High, the great King over all the earth!"

Psalm 47:2

The telephone rang for me last night. That's not a usual occurrence; lately the young men in my home occupy the phone. It was my tax preparer; it wasn't the news I desired. I will owe this year and it's a first. My tax preparer was so apologetic. I didn't get upset or nervous. I told him it could be so much worse. After our conversation there was a deep peace. This must have been the peace that passes all understanding. God is with me. I remember thinking a year ago this would have truly upset me. My stomach would have been in knots for a year.

I desire to be like that in all circumstances. Is that your desire also? Or are we not so much alike? Yes, I know that we all have distinct characteristics and are quite unique, financially our struggles may differ—but I'm speaking about something a little different. I am not sure my vocabulary is expansive enough to even explain it. There's something going on in the core of my being that says:

Hey, shouldn't you be operating on a higher plane, in a place where things no longer shake you up? Where nothing disturbs you, because you know that in times past God has been a mighty sustainer! Go on and do what the Lord has for you.

Well, generally there's a laundry list of concerns that are not visible to you, but seem to move with me wherever I am. Some days the list is annoying because it weighs heavy on the shoulders, and in my pockets. The list was so elaborate it could have been a shawl. How do you maneuver yours? I might be in the middle of a work meeting, church service or at the gas station—and the dreaded laundry list of concerns surfaces and I drag it along. My laundry list of concerns covers everything from my mom's arthritis (who is twelve hours away) to the cost of my son's future college tuition. My list is even departmentalized. Today, yes this very fine morning I believe the list was laid down maybe on the dashboard. I don't know. I am determined not to let my list overtake me. I want my joy cup back. No, I can not exchange my list, nor does anyone want it. I can't wish it away. But this morning I choose to focus on the higher things of God. Today I am walking in all of my abundance of peace, joy and love. I might not meet the deadline for my water bill, but Jesus gives me His good grace and it always works out.

Our Heavenly Father wants us to remember and

"…Be still, and know that I am God…" (Psalm 46:10)

Our God is sovereign and that alone should usher joy into our lives. So for now crumple up your laundry lists and:

"Clap your hands, all you nations; shout to God with cries of joy. How awesome is the Lord Most High, the great King over all the earth!"

Psalm 47: 1,2

Have a joyful day. Bless you.

BACK TO BASICS

"Let the wise listen and add to their learning, and let
the discerning get guidance"

Proverbs 1:5

I *t's not until we feel that we deserve better out of life, that our lives become better.*

Where did that thought come from? I asked myself that question. Nope, I didn't get an answer. That's what came to my mind, just as clear as day. It was a pronounced thought that resonated in my spirit. Oh sure the thought was simplistic, and to many of us it seems elementary, easy right? Then why are so many people silently suffering making the same mistakes over and over—trying to make sense of things, trying to work 'things' out independent of God, ignorant of Jesus and his masterful capabilities, attempting to get their lives in order. Unfortunately, when taken the independent route of the deity, the order never quite lines up with the plan. They say, "I'm getting it together." but the truth is their dashed dreams and misguided hope overtake them. Life is too much for them to handle on their own.

Is that why so many times we feel we've failed, when we've really pushed God out of our plans and then say, "I don't feel Him?" and "I can't see Him?"

Friends, I understand, it seems to make sense now that we need to get back to the basics! But what are the basics Lord? *I am sure* God will reveal the basics as the devotional unfolds.

This morning as I ate my breakfast, I began to regret not speaking to my cousin more in depth. He had phoned me in distress, crying because he needed to get away from his girlfriend. So he said. He said he loved her and decided to move to a small town in South Carolina (I had never known existed) and nothing was going according to his plan. My husband spoke to him and knew instantly what the problem was. Sure it might have been the girlfriend, but there were some terrible mistakes my cousin had found himself a part of.

While up stairs I hadn't heard the phone ring, in my haste, my mind had been reeling from my impending to do list. Then I heard my husband's voice; he called my name in a strange tone telling me that there was an emergency call from South Carolina. I had no idea who that could be. I quickly retrieved the telephone receiver and listened to an agonizing voice. I knew instantly it was my dear cousin, whom I truly loved. We are first cousins, there's family history. In our adult life we've only spoken sporadically, but each time I was delighted to hear his masculine but kind tone. I would always encourage him to seek employment or an educational opportunity and then share the locations of these empowering resources. When I spoke to him, I could hear my mother's encouraging qualities in my voice. I didn't verbally beat him up about his life choices, his approaching middle age and the need for a life altering change.

My cousin needed our immediate attention, and his life is suffering (Now you know, Jesus, can be that life altering answer. In time that solution will come).

What good would standing on a sanctimonious soapbox do now?

Instead, we encouraged my cousin, purchased a bus ticket, and directed him to go and seek loving help from our friends, Minister James Giles, Pastor Anthony and Sister Katherine Brown in Buffalo. These wonderful friends of ours have created a ministry that makes your heart swell with pride. This life-changing ministry gladly receives anyone desiring help to abandon a life defeating cycle. This ministry is aptly named Back to Basics, anyone, no matter your race, gender, station in life; their doors are open to all who have stumbled, made some heartbreaking decisions, done some hurtful things to themselves and others and need help and desire to have a relationship with Jesus Christ. Those that allow themselves to become involved in the ministry are never the same! God literally turns these former drug users, abusers, ex-felons, and whosoever desires to transform their life through a healing touch is welcomed to join this ministry. Ministry participants become healed men and women of faith.

I would like to hope that my cousin is tired of the draining dead-end lifestyle and is seeking a spiritual respite from his past life. We have witnessed people who came seeking answers and found the Back to Basics Ministry. This ministry has a divine power source, a Holy hook up that takes the fallen sinner, and dusts them off, prays over them, forgives them, mentors them, and nurtures them with the "love of Jesus."

So I shared this with you to say that often some of our choices put us in harms way, a slow walk into a mental and spiritual cess-pool, but never the less there is hope! Never the less we can run but we can't hide! The enemy plans for our trials to defeat and kill us. You'd think Satan would have it figured out by now; he can't stand up to the mighty arm of God. Sure my cousin might be running, I don't know, but experience says if he allows these down times to be teaching times, they can provide him with the Holy Ghost drawing power God uses to get our attention.

Friends, I am confident that when God intends for us to be a part of his kingdom building exercises, He'll plant you where and when He chooses. It's that divine timing that we weren't in on!

God knew we would be home yesterday morning when my cousin made his distress call. Surely we'd help, but more impor-tantly we'd point him in the direction of some loving arms, a ministry that would provide him with getting back to basics. Oh yes, I know some of the deep pain and hurt my cousin faced as a young teen, trying to sort out the why's and how comes of growing up without his natural parents, getting involved in a life that would lead to being in an out of prison—but if he really examines his life in his crippled spiritual and foggy mental state—he'll get the message that he has victory, there is still hope.

> "In this you greatly rejoice, though now for a little while
> you may have had to suffer grief in all kinds of trials.
> These have come so that your faith of greatest worth than
> gold, which perishes even though refined by fire-may be
> proved genuine and may result in praise, glory and honor,
> when Jesus Christ is revealed"

> I Peter 1: 6,7

I pray that my cousin in his crisis got on that bus, and could hear God talking to him all the way back to Buffalo, New York. I pray that he will be receptive to this ministry where God will sweetly provide healing and restoration for his weary mind, soul and spirit—*If he'll only receive it, if he'll only trust God first.*

Will you know where to direct someone that needs to get back to the basics of Holy living? Find out about the ministries in your community that empower the broken with Jesus! That's the back to basics they'll need. Keep that ministry directory handy, in arms reach; you'll never know when that distress call is coming.

> "But I call to God, and the Lord saves me. Evening,
> morning and noon I cry out in distress, and he hears my
> voice. He ransoms me unharmed from the battle waged
> against me, even though many oppose me"

> Psalm 55:16–18

Have a good day!

Confidently Praying

"Do not be anxious about anything, but in everything, by prayer and petition, with thanksgiving, present your requests to God; And the peace of God, which transcends all understanding, will guard your hearts and your minds in Christ Jesus."

Phil. 4:6–7

What was the matter? My friend and I walked around the corner, for our daily before lunch walk. We're getting so good at it; we need to think about extending the walk. It really goes quickly now; we talk, laugh and commensurate all the way. This has become my favorite part of the workday routine. (Yes, I realize that it's not work.) We catch up on things around the office, but always end our home stretch with discussing matters of the heart.

My friend shared that she had a good cry this morning and it just wasn't any one particular concern that prompted this display of emotions. She just had a good cry. I said, "You must have needed it." Sure there were things on her plate that a good cry would warrant, but the tears came un-expectantly and unannounced, during work time at that! This opened the door for me to share that lately crying has become such an easy thing for me. Monday the tears flowed like a river for me. I tried to hold back the tears, it did not work.

Today, I opened my e-mail from my husband and there was a simply sweet note. He asked me what was wrong and ended the note with *friends4ever*. This made me cry. My mind has been cluttered with much too much. I have not been totally open with some things that are bothering me, some decisions that we need to make together, some concerns that we must get to the bottom of. More importantly, I have been lax in my prayer life. My focus has been work, financial obligations, my health, missing friends, wishing I could see my mother more and on and on.

I should be overjoyed that my husband has been called to seminary; my son is doing reasonably well in school. Math surely has improved! My stepdaughters are well-read and good students. My friend commented on my weight loss, I'm enjoying walking, so I feel better, but! That tiny word with such extraordinary implications, but! There is something gnawing at me. I am feeling like my life should be moving at another pace, that the things of life, should be just that—all-small stuff, inconsequential things. My cheery tone has hibernated. My disposition is not always kind and loving. My family says, "Lighten up!" But (there's that word again) I can't just ignore the obvious. Change is needed and it's needed now!

Sure I pray, talk to God and marvel at His awesome wonder. But, lately it's sandwiched in between bedtime, cleaning up the kitchen or washing a load of clothes and work obligations. My prayer time is hurried; it's quick and unscheduled. I must do more than what I am doing.

Last Sunday our Pastor gave such a clear message about getting alone with God. In no uncertain terms, I know that I must do this, especially now. Pastor Wherry said it on Sunday, and this Thursday it has hit me like a tone of bricks. I need to hear from God, so that He can use me and I can become in touch with what next steps I need to take.

Two o'clock must be the anointed work hour for me, because the connection is becoming clearer for me. I returned to my desk and wondered what God would reveal for today's devotion. Earlier this morning I read a devotional regarding stewardship and then quickly read Malachi before my coworkers milled in.

After they arrive reading a scripture, and soaking in the text becomes a great difficulty. What did stand out in my mind was the idea that many of us don't trust God enough to give back to Him anything, especially our lives and our money. Financially that's a risky proposition for many. Money represents security for many. So consequently, we have difficulty with tithing.

I know the benefits of tithing. God stretches my pay so incredibly, and He continually blesses in ways I could never have orchestrated. Tithing is easy for me, what is difficult is letting go of all my concerns for longer than the prayer that I am sending up. Oh I say I trust Him, but worrying indicates that I don't. I am ashamed to admit it, I worry a great deal. Obviously, I am not praying confidently. Are you?

Oh as I write this it's now beginning to take shape in my spirit. I now understand what I need to do. I am so sure you've grasped it. Malachi 3: 10 says if we trust God enough he'll reveal some wondrous things. The scripture's words are:

> "Bring the whole tithe into the storehouse, that there may be food in my house. Test me in this," says the Lord Almighty, "and see if I will not throw open the floodgates of heaven and pour out so much blessing that you will not have room enough for it."
>
> Malachi 3:10

Remember a moment ago I told you I returned to my desk? Well when I did, there on the cover of another inspirational reading were the words: *Praying with Confidence.* I thought yep, that's what I need more of. Then I popped in my WOW Worship cassette tape and listened to several worship songs. God would have me envision a time when I would get to Calvary Baptist Church (in Buffalo) with Bishop T. Anthony Bronner presiding over the worship experience. I would drive with break neck speed. The weather might be icy, snow up to your calves, it did not matter. I would get there faithfully for Morning Prayer and worship. I attended weekdays, before speeding to work, sometimes I would leave Calvary and the spirit was so high, worship so sweet—you knew you had encountered Jesus.

Praying then transformed my life. Much of what I prayed and asked God for I did not see. Fervently, praying and believing—that's where I was spiritually!

I then believed God for a faith filled husband; at the time I had none. My son was a teen and I knew the importance of my child seeing his mother in a loving relationship. Young men need loving male role models. I believed God would send an upright, caring 'father' figures for my son, my brothers had all relocated. The fact was there were no serious prospects. I believed God for restoration of my finances; the reality was my bills far exceeded my income. I then believed God for a new level of faith; daily my faith was building, but the tests kept coming. I then believed God for an opportunity to move and start a new life in a thriving place, where people who looked like me loved life and were succeeding. The cost of relocating was staggering, so moving would simply be on hold. I then believed God for everything and anything. During my prayer life and my morning sojourns to Calvary opportunities came and God's love opened door after door. I prayer confidently and God answered my prayers in His time.

Glory to God, don't you see friends? I do now. My prayer life has dwindled and so I am not always in tune and in touch with our Heavenly Father, instead of relying on Him self has taken over. My feelings are in control, my thinking and narrow view of life has me continually whirling. It's no wonder I cry.

Friends, I don't know where there is an early Morning Prayer, worship celebration in the community. I am sure there are plenty. But in the meantime, Let's get up early, read our bibles, and let Jesus do the talking. We will begin to believe Him and pray confidently! That's what I am sure God is ushering us to do. And hopefully when that flood of tears comes, it will be because we recognize once again that we can completely believe and trust God for His promise of peace, protection, presence and power. Come on let's thank Him and praise Him for right now.

Have a joy filled day!

Opening the Eyes of
Our Understanding

"I keep asking that the God of our Lord Jesus Christ,
the glorious Father, may give you the Spirit of wisdom
and revelation, so that you may know him better. I pray
also that the eyes of your heart may be enlightened in
order that you may know the hope to which he has
called you, the riches of his glorious inheritance in the
saints, and his incomparably great power for us who
believe. That power is like the working of his mighty
strength."

Ephesians 1:17–19

Today, I drove instead of my husband. We are not yet a two-car family. So this often creates a challenge. My husband of course doesn't see it that way, I am independent, and don't like waiting to be picked up. But today was an exception. I was not at home waiting for his return or standing in the lobby of work waiting to go home. This day I was the captain behind the wheel and there he sat in the passengers' seat. He leaned over and whispered so I could not hear him. This was another of his antics, I just laughed at him.

Laughter is good medicine. He then said, "Honey, I am going to use your devotional intros when I preach." This was more a declaration, than a question. I said, "Oh?" I learned that technique from my mother and grandmother. That doesn't mean they're necessarily in agreement with anything you've said. What they're doing is digesting the statement. Then I perked up and said, "Who gets the credit and how will it sound?"

Rickey began to speak in a most authoritative voice, mimicking a distinguished, eloquent orator. He spoke through pursed lips with his head tilted. Each word that he spoke had a nasal quality. Prior to his playfulness my husband had requested that I write a devotional about our move from Buffalo to Virginia. I told him I thought I had already done that. Then he chimed in and said,

"It started out with great anticipation, this move from a far away place."

I interrupted and said, "No it did not!"

And laughed at him because I then really understood that that was how he viewed our move from Buffalo to Norfolk. His interpretation was quite different from mine. Friends I believe that my husband has an adventurous spirit, caulked full of romantic, idealistic viewpoints. Yeah sure that's me, but I want to see the specs, what's the plan and time frame? I'd like to think that I have the grounded view on life. Later that day I'd learn something new about myself. Often Rickey will compare our move to the days of being a pioneer when families sought out new experiences and weren't afraid to venture out into new vistas. His mental images differ from mine considerably. I'm not in full agreement with his view. But we do conclude that God had exercised His mighty arm on our behalf.

If the truth be told I would say the following: and it would not be spoken so eloquently but as old folks say "plain spoken!"

So I told my husband that he could use any introduction he elected for his sermons and then stated:

- *If the truth be told I wished we had made this move a decade ago.*
- *If the truth be told I was scared to death about leaving my comfort zone.*

- *If the truth be told I wished it had not been such a financial strangle hold around our necks moving from one state to another.*
- *If the truth be told I missed my mother, family and friends terribly and was lonely a great deal of the time.*
- *If the truth be told I wondered initially if the move was your idea and not God's.*
- *If the truth be told I prayed but felt God was not moving fast enough.*
- *If the truth be told I loved our surroundings but wondered if we would have to move into something less desirable.*
- *If the truth be told I would have done our move so much differently. No way would I have driven for 14 hours and then moved my own things, including furniture and appliances into the house. No way no how.*
- *If the truth be told I would have given up my faith if it had not been for our friends, family, Bishop and Pastor Dwight Brown and Mt. Ararat family who heard our desperate cries and came to our rescue.*
- *If the truth be told your faith and conviction shamed me. You would always say don't tell me what God won't do! Tell me what you don't believe.*
- *If the truth be told it took a year before I knew that Virginia was my home.*

If the truth were told it took this writing to see that I only saw what I could see. I've come to understand that I was seeing with the natural eye. Friends it wasn't until I got out of God's way and let Him be the Almighty Counselor and Provider that He is; I could not appreciate the wonder of who is God is in this instance.

Our move turned out nothing like I believed it would. There was no greeting committee with a love offering and a chicken casserole. Instead when we first arrived at 8 p.m.; our water wasn't even turned on. (God would send the landlord by to shut on the water.) We drove up and had to unload an over packed truck, just the three of us. We were sweaty, irritable, hungry and excited. Our new home was beautiful, but I was feeling out of place and out of sorts. Where was this place that we would now call home?

New promises and new possibilities were always before us, but I was too focused on the lack; lack of job security, lack of friends, lack of family, and lack of funds and lack of enough personal faith.

During those months I couldn't seem to stop worrying and realize what marvelous thing God was doing on a continuous basis. Oh, I'd say, *thank you Jesus* after the delivery of gifts, food, and employment. But had I only said:

Praise God during the storm, just imagine how far along the spiritual journey I'd be?

And now as I sit here many months later (try over eighteen) and I can see how God kept us and blessed us. Friends my eyes are wide open now, my heart if filled to capacity with thanksgiving. Thanksgiving for my peace, health, for my family, for my life, for you, for my natural and spiritual gifts, a divinely lead journey and for my salvation!

If the truth be told our move was just as God would plan it! It was a move that only He could navigate, a perfect move that created my total reliance on Him!

That's our lesson today friends, that we cannot know what God has in store for us even with our well devised plans, we must simply trust Him, and choose to persevere under the trial or break under the pressure. There were days my faith was the size of a mustard seed, and my spiritual knuckles were bleeding from the tight grip, but God!

If the truth be told...

"Blessed is the man who perseveres under trial, because when he has stood the test, he will receive the crown of life that God has promised to those who love Him."

James 1:12

Have a good day while you hold on to our faith and pray for a greater vision to see and embrace God's plan His way.

Yes, This Too Is Divine Order

"The one who comes from above is above all; the one who is from the earth belongs to the earth, and speaks as one from the earth. The one who comes from heaven is above all."

John 3:31

Yesterday evening I sat for just a few minutes alone on the beach. Actually, I was sitting on our medium size cooler. The day had been a fun filled day at the beach with my step-daughters and good friend and her three children. We had had a time giggling at them make new friends, splash happily in the water, chase each other and them settle for a few moments to have a picnic lunch. My friend, Marlene and I balanced out what the other brought. For example I brought the ice water that seemed to leek out the thermos, but she provided the lemonade, I brought the sandwich fixings and she provided the munchies. It was a healthy assortment and more than enough. God had wonderfully stretched the food, and fun. His provision was ample. Prior to coming to the beach we even had to stop and buy a swimsuit for a neighbor's niece who also joined us. Everything was in divine order. We sighed because it was an outing that the kids needed as well as the adults.

There I sat alone, watching guard over our beach chairs, bags, shoes and an empty cooler that contained sand particles. All was neatly packed and ready to be returned to the van, but the kids needed the sand rinsed out of their suits, off their bodies and clothes placed back on. For a few moments my attention was diverted and I instantly began to marvel at this new dimension to the outing—an atmosphere of peace and tranquility. And there I sat in the midst of it!

My spirit said...*Holy! Thank You! Glory to God! For faithfulness that enables me to see, every morning!*

You know friends, I was just singing, "Thank You Lord" by Daryl Coley's *Live in Oakland-Home Again.* His lyrics had great meaning for me as I sat in my peace time moment:

"Thank you nobody could do you like you do me Jesus, I just want to say Glory to you. Thank you for everything that you've freely given to me! Bless your name Jesus! Glory to you Jesus! My soul cries Holy, My spirit says Glory! I want to thank you Lord! Glory bless you Lord!"

The sun was beginning to set, the beach goers were thinning out and an air of stillness seemed to pervade all of this space of open peace.

My level of gratitude soared; this ocean vista was not far from my home. No I was not on vacation. This was Saturday and it was early evening. How I wished I could have shared this moment with all of my loved ones. I just know our breathing would have become shallow and the rates of our heart rates slowed and blood pressure lowered. I was in awe of the waters beauty as the tides rolled rhythmically. This movement pushed the sand and created a new landscape. I appreciated how God had given me this unexpected gift of tranquility, and I was witnessing first hand divine order as the water ebbed and flowed. The view was mesmerizing and healing.

God knew I would need to have that mental imagery to grasp onto today. The orange sky with streaks of white clouds, the sun setting and the command of the ocean with its steel blue flow.

After church service, my family returned home to find our back door open. Someone who lived in my home had left this door open. No one wanted to admit this mistake, or deal the blame. There have been numerous conversations had with my family about opening the door and leaving it unlocked. Before I knew it I was engaged in a verbal sparring match with my teen stepdaughter. There she stood challenging me, and sarcastically repeating what I said in a most impolite manner. Her exaggerated eye rolling and neck swaying were unacceptable. I was having none of the negative attitude, but what instantly came to mind was the tragedy of a young women I had known, who left her doors open as she pulled in her grocery bags, drove her car around her apartment building's designated parking space and returned to her home to meet her untimely demise. This young women's family has struggled with this loss. So as I looked at this young, rebellious teen in my home, and thought what is this and why? Mentally, questions began to roll:

Why the behavior? Why the attitude in my home? Why on this particular Sunday? Why after such a great Saturday! Why Lord? Why? The answer is pretty clear-cut.

"Because, just because this too is the acceptable order." And I could imagine God saying, *here's another test and another trial.*

Many of these spiritual realities are beyond us. If you think for a minute friend that the enemy is going to sit back and let you bask in God's divine tranquility at home or on the beach, we are all in for a rude awakening.

The truth of the matter is that when chaos, upheaval, confusion come to visit our comfort zones, we should be anything but dismayed. Don't even be surprised. Hey let's try this move on for size—don't even become shocked. Don't do like I do and entertain the author of confusion with too much conversation, but retreat to your prayer closets and trust that God has it all worked out in his divine order.

Friends I would be a hypocrite if I told you that I had this business of dealing with disturbing behavior all worked out. Oh I can come up with some immediate solutions to remedy disruptive behavior. But my friend Evangelist Wilma Taylor believes that God has appointed this time for me as a labor of love to model and mold these children into God fearing, loving young women. God knows that so many of us are challenged with this perspective. But I am prayerful and encouraged that this time in my life is ebbing and flowing like the Atlantic Ocean that I just marveled at on Saturday. God speaks to us in peacetime and as well as the roar over the ocean. Those of us that can't fathom:

Why? Why must there be confusion and upheaval?

Well, friends we need to get over that thinking because it's in our midst whether it be in our trials of personal relationships or on a professional level. It does exist and it is real!

But take heart friends, there's good news, we who believe in Christ Jesus and have an advocate with the Father, which is the Holy Spirit that intercedes on our behalf. The spirit has lead me to encourage you to read the entire book of James in the New Testament instead of just pointing out one or two scriptures like James 1:12 the scripture chosen for this devotional.

My bible's commentary encourages believers in the gospel, that's us, to endure our trials and joyfully benefit from them. If I hadn't read it for myself I would have a difficult time writing and understanding this. The Book of James reminds us that a genuine faith is a tested and tried faith. Imagine that! James' concluding chapters focus on the prayer of faith.

God has just spoken to our hearts, read and discover each of the five chapters and let's be encouraged by the knowledge that:

"Brothers, as an example of patience in the face of suffering, take the prophets who spoke in the name of the Lord. As you know, we consider blessed those who have persevered. You have heard of Job's perseverance and have seen what the Lord finally brought about. The Lord is full of compassion and mercy."

James 5:10–11

Have a great day and be sure to sing through your trials and hold those peaceful images in your mind! Be blessed.

His Power at
Work Within Us

"I pray that out of His glorious riches he may
strengthen you with power through his Spirit in your
inner being…"

Ephesians 3:16

I searched high and low. Looked throughout my journals, piles
of paper, underneath my nightstand and in baskets. There was
no sight of the devotional that I had written some time ago. This
devotional was written to encourage our hearts about victoriously
embracing challenges and the "unexpected" things of life that we
perceive as uncomfortable.

I can't find the devotional, but I refuse to let that stop me
from our encouraging one another. Are you aware of the marvelous power that operates in you? You might be like me, we say it,
but often we question it with our hesitant life styles. Haven't you
been invited to be a guest speaker, return back to school, teach a
class, chair a committee, design a logo, lead a crusade, campaign
for "your cause", host a meeting, write a letter, start a business or
(you fill in the blank) and you were paralyzed because you convinced yourself that the challenge was much too much?

I would like to think that God said:

*Wait a minute have you forgotten my power that is at work
within you?*

So you agree we need some encouragement today in that
area of our lives. Let me see if I can find someone around my
house that is willing to demonstrate that?

God had shown me this so clearly during the past summer with our son Michael. He is now a junior in High School. Michael was recently enrolled in the summer component of *Upward Bound* at Norfolk State University. I really appreciate the commitment and dedication of the staff; they love the students and inform them upfront that they are preparing for excellence, excellence now, and excellence in college and excellence in their future professional endeavors.

Upward Bound provides the participants with a host of educational and social experiences. They stress academics, but are big on fun. I have literally watched my son grow in confidence. Socially he's well rounded and enthusiastically began convincing me to allow him to sign up for the social graces program during the summer component. I was not convinced that that was what he needed along with his other academic programming. I encouraged him instead to take the sign language class. I pointed out that he had a friend at church that was deaf and that it would probably be a valuable experience learning sign language. Michael was not convinced. *Too bad,* I thought. *I am the parent and I insist.*

Well friends to make a long story short, Michael did extremely well in the class. At the end of the summer an award banquet was held to recognize the student's achievement, salute the staff and highlight the various program components. The art display of Georgia O'Keefe replicas was impressive; the students did a fine job. I could easily see how the teacher spurred their creative juices. I was also impressed with the ballroom promenade with the participants dancing to Luther Vandross. The students danced and curtsied in their tuxes and ballroom gowns, but of course I don't have to tell you that I was really overjoyed when the young people did a signing tribute to the 911 victims, super star Aliyah (I'm sure I've misspelled her name) and Lisa 'Left Eye' Lopez and surprisingly guess who was a participant?

Yes, he was, Michael was one of several lead persons who was showcased. He signed to the song, "One Sweet Day." The lyrics were touching, but what moved me was the fact that my son was standing before my eyes doing something he had protested. I instantly reflected on our conversations weeks ago. He was determined he would not do what was uncomfortable; he was not going to challenge himself and felt that I had been unfair. But God directed me in another direction. This moment was the reassurance that I had done the right thing. Then what really was the defining moment was when Michael stepped out of the line and independently signed during this song. I wanted to shout Halleluiah! It was a struggle for him, but he got through it and did incredibly well. That evening he also received two awards, most improved in Reading and English. Can't you just see it friends? God was speaking, speaking in a spiritual volume and I as in tune.

How often have we talked ourselves out of a challenging moment, been out of tune with God and tied His hands?

What do I mean? I mean when we are afraid to step up and embark on an unfamiliar challenge we prevent God from doing what He loves and that's to bless us and to demonstrate at every plausible opportunity what *His Power at Work Within Us* can achieve.

God was showing off and I loved it. I knew that Michael was being stretched in a direction he knew nothing of. I knew God was using my son by demonstrating to me that I need not to be intimidated by any more unfamiliar or uncomfortable circumstances. I like my child must learn to trust God more and stop being scared of failure. Oh friends, He'll even put us out in front of everyone, so that others can see and learn by God's example. We are often the unwillingly vehicle that God desires to enable and use. Only He can show case your abilities and get the desired results that let you know it was only because of His power that is at work in you that is causing you to do what you are doing. Just reflect on those times in your life when God was showing you off and pushing you up front for the world to see. Be sure to remember to give Him the glory.

This message is relevant for all of us, many months later. I would like to believe that if we continue to do what we always have; we'll continue to get what we always got! That's a paraphrased quote from Comedian Jackie "Moms" Mabley. Our limited experiences, limit us. Oh, but if we only trust God to stretch us, and keep us, this new faith filled experience will richly bless us in ways we can't imagine. We are open to the divine outpouring of our awesome Heavenly Father who will provide us with:

- A new level of dependence on Him,
- A new level of confidence in our God given abilities and talents,
- A new level of loyalty for our Father's divine power and wisdom,
- A new level of understanding of whom you belong to and who's you are,
- A new level of love, love for a Father that breaks us out of ourselves and draws us closer to Him and his purpose for our lives!

And more importantly we will know that we know about *His Power at Work Within Us!*

Friends just ask Michael, he knows where the source of his power lies, in the Almighty. Have a blessed day!

"I pray that out of His glorious riches He may strengthen you with power through His Spirit in your inner being, so that Christ may dwell in your hearts through faith, And I pray that you being rooted, and established in love, may have power, together with all saints, to grasp how wide and long and high and deep is the love of Christ, And to know that this love that surpasses knowledge-that you may be filled to Now to Him who is able to do immeasurably more than all we ask or imagine, according to His power that is at work within us, to Him be glory in the church and in Christ Jesus throughout all generations, for ever and ever! Amen."

Ephesians 3: 16–21

On A Final Note...

Friends, I want to thank you for being a supportive and endearing travel companion with me, as we learned to take this life changing walk with Jesus in the Blessedness of Believing. I pray that you too believe God for everything; every possibility and seemingly impossibility that you are currently facing. As a result of our faith and God's grace we believe in all confidence that there is nothing to difficult for our God, our Mighty Heavenly Father, our Protector, our Deliverer and our Redeemer!

The Holy Spirit has prompted me to take another introspective look at my life before concluding this part of the journey. There was good reason that I couldn't ignore the feeling that surely there must be a greater victory than getting through the tug and pulls of daily living. Is there more in store for all of us? Indeed there is! On that final note, I feel compelled to share this with you.

In the past twenty-four hours I have read and heard some life changing news. This is another transition time in our lives, I sense it, feel it and can almost see it. This is far from over, but yet another season is concluding and another beginning. At approximately 4:00 a.m. I was unable to sleep, so instead of tossing and turning and playing the same old mental tapes, I sat straight up in my bed, turned on my lamp and reached for *The Spirit Led Woman*. (Go on Christ anointed/filled brothers substitute your gender in that title, you too are—*The Spirit Led Man!*) This thin devotional was tucked under many books, I picked up several unread novels, my journal and there it lay. I reached for *The Spirit Led Woman* as though I was looking intentionally for that. I had no idea what I would read, nor learn. I opened this book and discovered an article entitled *Seeing the Invisible*. I am sure God lead me to this book and this article, I knew immediately this message was from God and it impacted me greatly. Author Shirley Arnold had no idea that a woman in Norfolk, Virginia, would be so blessed at 4 a.m. with her writing. She spoke about how we are all embracing the Prayer of Jabeez, (and there is not a thing the matter with that) we recite the scripture and request that our territories be increased, but do we really have a handle on what each of our territories is? Her premise is that we very well might not have a proper view of our territories because our spiritual views are obstructed with anger, pain, hurt, the job, "the kids", and the list goes on. Those issues become our territories and we miss out on the bigger view! God desires that we see over our valley into larger, vistas with breathe taking views.

Then it was as though author Shirley Arnold was standing in my room and asked:

"Linda how is your view?"

Immediately, my spirit stood up and said that I have a sight problem. I was convicted and knew my view had been obstructed by my life's current set of circumstances and consequently, I was not seeing clearly—beyond confusion (last week, no yesterday if God had placed a flag pole in the middle of my yard I am sure I would have overlooked its majesty and worth!) I was farsighted and had no spiritual insight because I refuse to see beyond my feelings.

I thank God for his love, tender mercies and words of encouragement. The Author Shirley Arnold immediately brought them home to me right there at 4 a.m. Friends, God desires to change my spiritual view, and your spiritual view so that He can bless us in territories we can't imagine. Our spiritual growth is the key to this process. We must take a close and honest look at where we are in our walk with Jesus and are we seeing what He desires us to see and working towards that end or are we seeing what only we can see with the natural eye and walking in circles starting out in a defeated state. Ask him to provide you with corrective lenses if you need to have your vision altered.

Today, praise God from whom all blessings flow I have a new view, a better view, with daily application of God's word my vision should be cleared so I really see God's plan for my life. My territories will increase.

I also invite you to experience an increase in your territories. God changed my view and has begun to increase my territories through His mighty words in 2 *Kings* 6:15–17, *Isaiah* 42:6,7; *Matthew* 6:22–23; *Matthew* 13:10–17; *Mark* 8:22–25; 2 *Corinthians* 3:12–18.

After reading the article I slept like a baby. I thanked God and was assured that He needed me to know there was so much more in store for my territory, my spiritual inheritance, but I needed to step out of the valley and move up the mountain. With spiritual growth comes the truth. And the truth is there are painful areas in my life that I refuse to shout over any longer! How about you? So I awoke refreshed, determined to learn more and there it was friends, a commentary that said: "Take Time For The Pain" by Reverend Dr. James Forbes. The Holy Ghost has come to revive us again through this man of God who has said:

> *Jesus can handle the pain in our lives when we take time, when we bring it to him in faith. We have a responsibility to take time for the pain–the pain of our friends, our coworkers, and people in general. Every now and then we must stop and take care of our own pain. To do this we must:*
>
> *Face the pain in our lives, admitting its reality. It may be hard to face, but when we do, we can begin to work through it. We can live victoriously over it and not be mastered by it.*

Trace the source of the pain in our lives. Sometimes we need an objective, outside observer to pinpoint things we don't see or won't see in our lives.

Finally, we need to 'grace' the pain that is, put it in its proper place. Romans 8: 28 suggests that God uses pain and tribulation to make things right in our lives.

Paul talks about his own thorn in the flesh and how he asked God to remove it three times but God said, "My grace is sufficient for you, for my power is made perfect in weakness" (2 Corinthians 12:9). In effect, he says, "My grace will be with you in your fiery furnace, my grace will help you part the waters of your Jordan Rivers. My grace will shut the mouths of the lions in your lion's den. My grace will fight your battles and bring down the walls of your Jerichos'."

"What kind of pain are you facing in your life today? God is able to give you the strength to make it through, but you've got to take time for the pain."

Take Time For The Pain by Reverend Dr. James Forbes, pg. 1058. African-American Devotional Bible New International Version, Grand Rapids, MI: Zondervan Publishing House, 1997.

Praise God we are not alone on this grace filled Christian journey Friends! The winds of change have once again not only occurred in my life but in all of our lives. My stepdaughters: Mary, Taylor and Jaycina and son: Michael is acknowledging and experiencing God's blessings first hand with obtaining college scholarships, work study assignments and recipients of honors awards. It's music to all of our ears, when they report enthusiastically about their lives. Each of them actively is involved in social, spiritual and academic enrichment experiences in Charlotte, Washington,

D.C. and Buffalo. Mary is enrolled in a Nursing Program at North Carolina A&T State University. Yes, she has Aggie pride! Mike attends Shaw University; he's a scholar and student ambassador for his university. These young adults are visibly appreciative and happily displaying loving dispositions. Taylor is excelling and loving High School and Jay is an honors student, proud to be graduating. Yes, there is something wonderful occurring right before my eyes. Thank God I didn't abandon my divine mission. I would have missed all of this. Now, five years later, after my inception of my devotionals, I see that life continues to hold more and more promise! We've come to really value family relationships and know about the unspeakable complexity of grief through the untimely death of my stepson, Courtney. Friends, that same weekend of Courtney's burial and life celebration, my husband obtained his Master of Divinity Degree. God does provide us with olive branches. He pastors and passionately provides Clinical Pastoral Care as a Chaplin, ministering to many families who also are journeying a similar road of grief. Today, I share with you and joyfully celebrate the birth of this devotional work. Be assured that while we continue to move to higher spiritual heights and travel unknown roads we can be confident that God does honor His word and we are richly blessed! Take care.

BIBLIOGRAPHY

Arnold, Shirley. *Seeing The Invisible Spirit led Woman Empowered For Purpose.* Lake Mary, Florida: Strang Communications Company, 2002.

Author Unknown. 2000. *Our Daily Bread.*

Bennett, V. Harold. "What Makes the Body Work." *The African-American Devotional Bible* (NIV). Michigan: Zondervan, 1997.

Blackaby, Henry T. *Created To Be God's Friend: How God Shapes Those He Loves.* Nashville: Thomas Nelson Publishers, 1999.

Ezell, Susan Dale. *Living Simply in God's Abundance, Strength and Comfort for the Seasons of A Woman's Life.* Nashville: Thomas Nelson Publishers, 1998.

Forbes, Reverand Dr. James. "Take Time for the Pain." *The African-American Devotional Bible* (NIV). Michigan: Zondervan, 1997.

Hughes, Langston. *The Collected Poems of Langston Hughes, ed.* Rampersad, Arnold and Associates. ed. Roessel. David, New York: Vintage Books, 1994.

Hunter, Millicent Dr. Strong. *Medicine Prescriptions for Successful Living.* New Kensington, Pennsylvania: Whitaker House, 2001.

Joy For The Journey: A Woman's Book of Joyful Promises. Dallas, Texas: Word Publishing Inc., 1997.

Ormon, Stormie. *The Power of a Praying Wife.* Oregon: Harvest House Publishers, 1997.

Stanley, Charles. 2002. *In Touch Magazine.*

Sortor, Toni and McQuade. *Prayers & Promises.* Ohio: Barbour Publishing, Inc. 2001.

Taylor, Wilma Evangelist. *Wilma Taylor Ministries of Chicago, Illinois*

Williams, Bishop Milton A. "Expect the Unexpected." *The African-American Devotional Bible* (NIV). Michigan: Zondervan, 1997.

BIBLES

African-American Devotional Bible New International Version. Grand Rapids, Michigan: Zondervan Publishing House, 1997.

www.Blue Letter Bible.Com

Good News Study Bible with Deuterocanonicals/Apocrypha: Today's English Version. New York: American Bible Society, 1993.

Holy Bible King James Version: The Open Bible Edition. Nashville: Thomas Nelson Publishers, 1975.

The Full Life Study Bible: An International Study Bible for Pentecostal and Charismatic Christians New International Version. Life Publishers International, 1992.

The Parenting Bible Christian Values for Today's Family, New International Version. Grand Rapids, Michigan: Sanderson Publishing House, 1994.

MUSICAL INSPIRATION

Alicia. "We Win." 2001.

Adams, Yolanda. "More Than a Melody." 1995.

Cleveland, James. "You Didn't Bring Me This Far to Leave Me."

McClurkin, Donnie. "DM, Speak To My Heart." 1990.

McClurkin, Donnie. "Live In London." 2001.

The Mississippi Mass Choir. "It Remains To Be Seen." 1993.

Winans, CECE. "Alone In His Presence Praise Medley (Psalms 150)." 1995.

Quiet Times. "Inspirational CD" Kelly, R. "I Believe I Can Fly." 1996.